W9-CFU-322

IMAGINING HOME

Imagining
Home

Writing from the Midwest

Mark Vinz and Thom Tammaro
editors

University of Minnesota Press
Minneapolis
London

Copyright 1995 this collection by the Regents of the University of Minnesota

All rights reserved. No part of this publication may be reproduced, stored in a retrieval system, or transmitted, in any form or by any means, electronic, mechanical, photocopying, recording, or otherwise, without the prior written permission of the publisher.

Published by the University of Minnesota Press
111 Third Avenue South, Suite 290, Minneapolis, MN 55401-2520
Printed in the United States of America on acid-free paper

Library of Congress Cataloging-in-Publication Data
Imagining home : writing from the Midwest / Mark Vinz and Thom
   Tammaro, editors.
      p.   cm.
   ISBN 0-8166-2780-0 (hc)
      1. American literature—Middle West.   2. Authors, American—Homes
and haunts—Middle West.   3. Place (Philosophy)—Literary
collections.   4. Middle West—Literary collections.   5. American
literature—20th century.   6. Home—Literary collections.   I. Vinz,
Mark, 1943– .   II. Tammaro, Thom.
PS563.I46   1995
810.8′03277—dc20   95-18078

The University of Minnesota is an
equal-opportunity educator and employer.

Contents

Introduction

The question of a particular locale's influence on an individual is indeed a complex one, for, as the essays in this collection emphasize again and again, *place* is far more than a matter of geographical landscape. Rather, it is an emotional complex of associations, both generative and restrictive; it is the human communities that inhabit landscapes—their attitudes and values, their particular (and sometimes peculiar) ways of arranging and expressing themselves and relating both to each other and "the outside." Place, too, has something to do with history itself, and the ways the past can or cannot be accessed by memory; with ancestry, and the dynamics created by the confluence of the personal and the collective; with spirituality, in all its formal and informal guises; and always, with inevitable change, both inner and outer. Especially for a writer, it is what one cannot go back to yet indeed must go back to, for therein lies the source of much that is vital to the writing itself. As Larry Watson remarks in his essay "When Everybody Wore a Hat," "We can go home again, but the only paradise is the paradise lost."

In the process of editing our first anthology of midwestern writing, *Inheriting the Land: Contemporary Voices from the Midwest* (University of Minnesota Press, 1993), we solicited comments from a number of writers regarding the ways *place* had influenced their development—and many of those comments stayed with us. The more we thought about it, the more we wanted to return to those kinds of responses, in a format that would encourage both thorough and varied exploration—of the sort we had found in another collection of essays published by the University of Minnesota Press, and which both of us had used as a text in our classes, *Growing Up in Minnesota*, edited by Chester G. Anderson, as well as in *Growing Up in the Midwest*, edited by Clarence A. Andrews (Iowa State University Press). It was a combination of our desire to extend what we found in the Anderson and Andrews books and our own editorial attempts to examine other writers' responses to questions of *place* that became the chief motivation for embarking on this essay project.

What we decided to seek from a group of writers whose poetry, fiction, and nonfiction we admire involved both focus and variety. The focus arises from the question—perhaps even a directive—we posed to each writer in this anthology: to explore the ways in which the midwestern landscapes of their lives, past and present, have influenced their thinking and writing; to confront directly the ways in which the landscapes of the particular geographical territory we have sought to explore—the Upper Midwest, the northern tier of states from the Great Plains to the western Great Lakes—have shaped their attitudes, values, sense of the past, and development as writers. We have felt that although the topography varies considerably in the Upper Midwest, there is nonetheless a kind of cohesiveness—perhaps from the relative lack of large urban centers in the region, perhaps because of the low density of population, perhaps because of its distance from the South's influences so noticeable in the southern part of the Midwest. As Michael Martone indicates in "The Flyover," there are indeed *real* differences within the greater Midwest; but also, aside from a few places such as the Mall of America, not many know where to locate it. Perhaps because of "the area's own invisibility to itself," appellations such as "Upper" or "Eastern" have become necessary definers. This has something, of course, to do with the extremes of weather ("all weather and not much else," Patricia Hampl says of her childhood perceptions of St. Paul), but with other kinds of extremes, too, and the tensions between them: mundane and obvious versus complex and mysterious, "barren and flat and full of Bibles" (as Jack Driscoll was once warned) versus richly subtle and endlessly variable—and even "poetic" and "romantic." Whatever the Upper Midwest is, the perception of it certainly arises from a combination of factors—which both of us have experienced living in Minnesota, as well as in making the transition from Kansas and Indiana, the other places we've lived in the larger region. And of the perceptions themselves, we well know that they remain a matter of *seeing*—landscape itself, as Patricia Hampl also says, "plays a key role in the formation of the imagination"—a way, finally, to come to terms with "the paradox of love and disdain in one's home place."

Among other things, American literature has always been a literature preoccupied with region and place: the South of William Faulkner, Flannery O'Connor, Eudora Welty, and Zora Neale Hurston; the New England of Robert Frost, Sarah Orne Jewett, E. A. Robinson, and May Sarton; the Midwest of Sherwood Anderson, Willa Cather, F. Scott Fitzgerald and Meridel Le Sueur; the Southwest of Edward Abbey, Rudolfo Anaya, N. Scott Momaday, and Leslie Marmon Silko; the West of Wallace Stegner, John Steinbeck, Robinson Jeffers, and Gary Snyder; the Pacific Northwest of Raymond Carver, Richard Hugo, Carolyn Kizer, and William Stafford.

Many excellent studies have explored the relationship of place and landscape in the work of American writers, among them Elaine and William Hedges's *Land and Imagination: The Rural Dream in America* (1980), Alfred Kazin's *A Writer's America: Landscape in Literature* (1988), and Frederick Turner's *Spirit of Place: The Making of an American Literary Landscape* (1989). Studies of the Midwest in particular begin as early as Ralph Rusk's *The Literature of the Middle Western Frontier* (1925) and continue to the present with such collections and studies as John J. Murray's *The Heritage of the Middle West* (1958); Thomas McAvoy's *The Midwest: Myth or Reality?* (1961); Robert Killoren's *Late Harvest: Plains and Prairie Poets* (1977); James Shortridge's *The Middle West: Its Meaning in American Culture* (1989); David Pichaske's *Late Harvest: Rural American Writing* (although not exclusively Midwest in scope, 1991); and most recently, Ronald Weber's *The Midwestern Ascendancy in American Writing* (1992). We are also pleased to hear that the Society for the Study of Midwestern Literature—headquartered at Michigan State University—is currently developing the *Dictionary of Midwestern Literature* project, which should draw a new and interesting literary map of the territory.

So while there exists a respectable body of scholarship *about* the literature of place and landscape—and specifically about the literature and landscapes of the Midwest—there are fewer collections in which these issues are addressed by writers themselves.

This collection of essays, then, attempts to explore the confluence of writer and his or her landscape. All of the writers here have used the midwestern landscapes of their childhood and adulthoods as both background and foreground to their fiction, poetry, and essays, so the territory we invited them to explore was not totally new to them. We hoped the essays would focus more on the impact of the landscape and nature on the writer than on nature writing per se. We asked our writers to adjust their angle of vision for a moment—or at least for an essay's moment. And we are pleased that they so eagerly took up the challenge.

As for the variety we sought in authors' responses, we have been more than amply rewarded. Obviously, when we commissioned these authors to write original essays for this collection, we could neither predict nor govern what they would say. We hoped our focus would offer them the flexibility of imagination and style to approach the subject, yet also in some way tether them to it. We selected these writers not only because we admire their work, but also because we were confident that they would think deeply and seriously about the parameters of the "assignment" (as one of the authors called her essay).

Indeed, as we have read and reread the essays, and worked with the authors in shaping them, we've been particularly struck by the richness of the work.

While this is partly defined by the diversity of places and times written about, it is also a matter of wonderfully individual voices: from angles of approach and emphasis—at times oblique and idiosyncratic—to sources of meaning and direction. The mixture seems enriched by the fact that some of these authors—Jack Driscoll, Kathleen Norris, and Robert Schuler, for example—are not native Midwesterners or Upper Midwesterners, and still others—such as Martha Bergland, David Haynes, Michael Martone, and

Mary Swander—have lived in more than one place within the larger region. (Indeed, while David Haynes has lived for many years in St. Paul, his focus is surburban St. Louis, the one locale in this collection that slips outside our geographic parameters but nonetheless reflects an urban midwestern experience.) Likewise, although some of these writers have already distinguished themselves in the genre of the essay—Carol Bly, Paul Gruchow, Bill Holm, Kathleen Norris, and Linda Hasselstrom come to mind—for others, such as Martha Bergland, Jack Driscoll, Jon Hassler, Robert Schuler, and Larry Watson, the form has provided a relatively new and challenging experience. No matter what the background of the individual authors may be, nor the manner in which they approached the topic of *place*, we've been both delighted and made thoughtful by what we've read—that, more than anything else, is what we hope to pass on to readers.

For all of the diversity we have encountered, a kind of ordering principle has also emerged. There are indeed several possible ways of presenting the work, emphasizing both the variety and commonality of its themes and approaches, but one in particular has interested us.

One group of writers (Michael Martone, Robert Schuler, Mary Swander, Kathleen Norris, and Jack Driscoll) emphasizes what it means to be transplanted to the Upper Midwest, and the different ways of finding a home here. Another group (Martha Bergland, Jon Hassler, David Haynes, David Allan Evans, Larry Watson, and Patricia Hampl) focuses on the power of place and memory in another way—in terms of ancestry and what has been recovered in the process of memory's stewardship. Finally, a third group (Paul Gruchow, Linda Hasselstrom, Carol Bly, Bill Holm, and Kent Meyers) is particularly interested in the changes that have occurred (both within and without) as an inevitable part of the Upper Midwestern experience—in some of the larger social issues that surround those changes, and in the kinds of reassessments the individual must make as a result.

In "Corn Village," one of her great elegiac essays about the Midwest—and Kansas, specifically—Meridel Le Sueur writes, "Not going to Paris or Morocco or Venice, instead staying with you, trying to be in love with you, bent upon understanding you, bringing you to life. For your life is my life and your death is mine also." This might well serve as an epigraph for this collection. These writers have stayed with the Midwest: loving it; hating it; wrestling with its contradictions, its transparency, its opacity, its ambiguity; but ultimately moving to embrace it. To the degree that a writer's personal truth reflects a universal truth, we hope, finally, that these sixteen essays will offer readers a starting point for exploring and discovering how the landscapes of their own homes have been a shaping influence in their lives.

We would like to express our appreciation to many people who have worked with us and supported us in their various good ways to shape this book: to Moorhead State University for Release Time Awards, which provided us valuable time to complete the manuscript; to Sheila Coghill and Betsy Vinz for their encouragement and support along the way; to Ron Gower and Jill Gidmark, who read early versions of our proposal and offered insightful commentary; to Beverly Kaemmer, our editor, and the staff at the University of Minnesota Press, who brought this book to life.

One writer we initially considered approaching for this collection was Frederick Manfred, but his failing health would make it impossible for him to contribute. On September 9, 1994, at the age of eighty-two, Fred died in a Luverne, Minnesota, hospital, longing to return to "Roundwind," the house he'd built from native rock in the heart of the mythical "Siouxland" that anchored so much of his writing. Fred's more than forty books of fiction, poetry, and nonfiction alone are enough to carve out his place in midwestern and American literature. But, what is more important, Fred was father and friend and supporter to so many writers in the Midwest. His presence will be truly missed.

And so it is to Frederick Manfred, Creator of Landscapes, Imaginer of Home, that we dedicate this book.

Mark Vinz / Thom Tammaro
Moorhead, Minnesota

Discovering a Home

The Flyover

Michael Martone

How did I know it was finally spring? This was in May, in Ames, Iowa. I was teaching at the university there. Between the administration building and the agriculture hall, in the middle of the campus, there is a ten-acre field that once had been a sheep meadow when the college was simply the state experimental farm. That meadow is now landscaped with all the trees and bushes indigenous to the state. I had heard that Frederick Law Olmsted, the architect of Central Park, had designed the plantings, but I could never prove it, such claims for his work being as common as the beds Washington was claimed to have slept in. In any case, the central campus was gorgeous, the flowering crab apples and dogwoods set against the oaks and freshening conifers with clumps of crocuses blooming at their feet. The grass looked painted green, the sun high enough in the sky at last to swab a shadow of the campanile, in a darker green, across it. Students lounged on the lawn using their books as pillows.

Still, these signs alone were not enough to convince me of the turn of the season. Having lived there only a few years, I had witnessed late winter storms howling in a wind the natives say blows there all the way from the

Copyright 1995 by Michael Martone

Rockies because there is nothing to get in the way. The sign I looked for was more superstitious, more magical. And there it was, the university's maintenance crews out on the lawn tearing down the snow fences, those pickets of cedar staves and twisted wire designed to knock down the wind's speed enough for the snow to drop out of the gale and drift away from the walkways. The snow fences, constructed in the fall, crisscrossed the campus. It always seemed to me they were like the decoy airplanes the cargo cults built on South Sea islands. The fences worked better, however. They inevitably attracted the snow. Now that they were being rolled up, I could relax, stretch out, and look up at that blue and endless sky above this part of the world.

The blue is so big you are convinced you can see the sky bend, shading in the periphery of your vision as in the deep folds of silk. In Iowa, in the Midwest, one watches the sky a lot. You are drawn to its vastness, to your easy access to it, not just for the weather that actually delivers something to you and your neighborhood, but for the narrative the sky generates and transmits. You read it. Tune it in like another band of the radio waves it also serves as a medium to transport. The colors, the wind, the clouds pour over you scudding to the east, swimming upstream against the advancing sunlight. A film loop that never stops running from horizon to horizon, a ticker tape, a scroll.

There I was on that spring day once again reading the sky. Immediately, I saw in the air above Iowa the vapor trails of jets blooming behind the pinhead twinkle of the planes miles above me. On those days when the skies are cloudless, you can count ten or twelve flights streaking over, sketching out a corduroy weave to the sky. As one long arching cloud finally evaporated, two or three more were growing nearby, east to west, west to east. The planes crept back and forth, strangely mirroring the trajectory of tractors here on earth. They plowed the sky, turning over the blue field, leaving a furrow of jumbled and chunky clouds. The contrails hung there, it seemed, forever, and as they overlapped and smeared slightly in the prevailing wind, the sky, a cold clear glass, suddenly frosted with spiky fingers of water forming crystals.

As a Midwesterner, I have thought, on those lazy afternoons looking up at the sky, what this place must look like from the air. Of course, I, myself, have been a passenger staring through the double-paned plastic window of a 737, noting the signature of the township grid, the rumpled patchwork quilt of the land. But most often I find myself as the observer stuck on the ground. This perspective suits me best, appropriate perhaps for one from this part of the planet. Perhaps as appropriate, I can't help projecting myself up to those planes. I adopt that point of view for the quarter hour the plane takes to stretch by overhead. Then I come back to earth.

I can't help but think of my earthbound state. After all, I know there are people riding by above me who consider this place, the Midwest, and the people who inhabit it "the Flyover," meaning to dismiss it, of course, as just an empty space that holds the two coasts apart. And those busy planes do seem as if they are conducting important missions as they stride over us, inscribing their paths on the sky like those looping lines the airlines themselves draw on their route maps of the United States. Look, those charts seem to say, an easy hop, skip, and jump over all this blank space.

Sometimes, I believe this implied message and the busy air traffic of people going places graphically illustrates the concept. But more often I think that those passengers above don't know what they are missing. With that in mind, I would wrap those lovely spring days around me, keeping what I know of this place a secret. Let altitude then be the best defense and let the Midwesterner wear the mantle of "the Flyover" as a kind of camouflage. Down below I'll be waving, waving, glad to see those above rush by, taking with them those streaked mental snapshots they've recorded from their cramped coach seats as souvenirs of the Midwest and their few minutes above us.

The truth is that such an ambiguous feeling about the Midwest seems to me to be very midwestern. Simultaneously, a Midwesterner can imagine himself mired at the end of the earth and ensconced at its very heart. The conflict between the ideals of community and mobility has long been a central drama of America itself, but only in the Midwest, it seems to me, is this drama expressed so subtly and engrossingly. If the rest of Americans know anything about this region they know it as the place where something or someone is *from*. Midwesterners themselves have a harder time simply saying where this place is.

Let's say that Ohio, Indiana, Michigan, Wisconsin, Minnesota, North Dakota, South Dakota, Nebraska, Kansas, Missouri, Illinois, and Iowa will make up our flyover. My students in Iowa always excluded Ohio and Michigan from their maps of the Midwest as Eastern States. Growing up in Indiana, I would never include Missouri, too southern, or Kansas, too western, in my cognitive setup. I bet if you ask a resident of any of our target states they would affirm without question that the ground they are standing on is pure midwestern soil. They might go on then and amend the appellation, Midwest, with "Upper" or "Eastern" to fit in those other states. Or ask them of the region's identifying characteristic. You will probably get a description of a "typical" midwestern state that matches the habitat of your informant's. The Midwest *is* farming and small towns if you are from Iowa, not just any old farming but corn farming. From Indiana, I always thought a mixture of medium-sized industrial cities and small farms were needed as the ingredients of any midwestern composition. That's the rub. No one really knows where or what the Midwest is. We could argue all day about its geography, its demographics, heck, even its ethos. My definition, finally, evolved to incorporate that basic mystery, the area's own invisibility to itself. No one knows for sure where it is, but everyone is sure it is great to be from there.

Photographs taken from the air offer us something between these two extreme views of the Midwest. Rendered here is not the smear of terrain seen from the jet stream. Nor is it the close-up view that attempts to capture the essence of the Midwest. The Midwest, because it is so vast and diverse, is largely invisible, not only to those rushing through it or over it, but even to those who live within its borders. The Midwest is hidden in plain sight. Often, those of us who live here have grown used to the subtle and varied pleasures of this home and have come to think of where we live as a basal line of experience from which the extremes of other regions spike above and below our expectations. For bicoastal travelers, this angle of imaging adds a discriminating lens to their bird's-eye view. But for Midwesterners this angle provides a platform from which to observe ourselves and our surroundings, perhaps for the first time. It gives us just enough distance to picture ourselves without stepping out of the picture all together.

There are the old jokes, blackout sketches, and cartoons about the amateur photographer with a Brownie camera taking group pictures at a certifiably photogenic locale, the Grand Canyon, say, or Big Sur, Pikes Peak or the Everglades, and being so involved with the composition of the image in the viewfinder that he directs his subjects or himself off the nearby cliff or back into the swampy water. Imagine now such a setup in the Midwest. The photographer, chances are, could tell his whole extended family to take a step back for almost forever and, most times, never approach the lip of any danger.

An aerial shot of the Grand Canyon is just another spectacular picture. Some things are easy to see. The Midwest is hard to see, especially when you are in it. In the photos we take of ourselves, we tend to think of the background of where we live as just that, background. Our families, our friends are most often our subjects. The background is seldom, if ever, a picture in its own right. It isn't one we keep. Those other pictures, those thrilling vistas, we believe are somewhere else. Perhaps that is why so many of us can't imagine missing that background until we've moved away or why I project myself up to the clouds to get some perspective. The perspective of hovering seems necessary, a way to build a mountain view into the plains and prairies, the still lakes and rolling hills we think we know like the backs of our hands.

Living in a flat land, I have always wanted to be able to gaze down on the world. Chicago obliged. My earliest memories are of taking trips to Chicago, the birthplace of the skyscraper, and climbing to the observation decks of the tall buildings. First, there was the Standard Oil Building near the lake where I thrilled each time a little airplane settled on Meigs Field below. From up there, I imagined, you could see the lakeshore curve all the way back to Indiana, and from there I watched the cranes and construction workers stitch together the X's of the Prudential Building going up. And once that building was finished, from the platform there, do I remember looking down at the Standard Oil Building where I once stood? From the

Prudential Building, I could see, close up, the fine detail of the Tribune Tower and the Wrigley Building and stare at the hypnotic rhythm of the Corn Cobs near the river where, nearby, the asymmetrical shafts of black glass raced each other to be the top of the Sears Tower. From that observation deck, every time I'd be there, I would call home from one of the pay phones. All the towers have a radio station broadcasting from their peaks. As I'd talk with my folks, I could read the deejay's lips in his glass booth, both of us hoping our messages would convey our new take on the world. The sky, in my memory, always severely clear, opened up forever. Only the earth's gentle curve ever obstructed the view. From the angle of the observation deck you can make up a kind of sense of what's below. You want to share it with as many people as you can. Once I watched a fleet of helicopters lift off from Grant Park, and a president and his entourage thundered by at eye level on the way to O'Hare. Up there, I could get closer than any parade route on the ground.

As I think about the Midwest as the Flyover, I find myself thinking about flight in general. Perhaps you wouldn't associate the Midwest with flying. After all, this region seems relentlessly earthbound. There is so much of it. Then again, what region could be more fertile in creating the daydreams of flight? I'm not the first Midwesterner who has felt the tug of gravity and conjured up ways to escape it. As I said, we are of two minds, or better yet two mediums, rooted down to earth and with our heads in the clouds. Many places in the Midwest are connected to the seemingly indifferent flight paths that arch above them. Let me map a constellation of aviation shrines. I'll do my own flyover of the territory covered here, an acrobatic touch-and-go on the route our reconnaissance planes have taken.

Beginning in Ohio, we discover the Wright brothers themselves in their Dayton bike factory. There, now, is the Air Force Museum with its huge hangarlike building that is still not large enough to house the sparkling B-36. And up the road is Wapakoneta, where Neil Armstrong was born. His own moon-shaped museum looks as if it is in close synchronous orbit, floating a few feet above a green Ohio hillock. In Indiana, where the Wright brothers were born and Armstrong went to school, Purdue University, the alma mater of astronauts, once owned Amelia Earhart's Lockheed Electra. She was still a member of the faculty when she disappeared in the Pacific. In Michigan, Ford built the famous Tri-Motor, and, when he couldn't get the real thing for his museum in Greenfield, collected the replica of the *Spirit of St. Louis*, the one that Jimmy Stewart flies in the movie. Across Lake Michigan in Wisconsin, Oshkosh hosts its annual fly-in with its home-built craft that look again like bicycles with wings the Wright brothers could have built. Experimental planes made out of laminated graphite, ancient biplanes, GeeBees jam the summer sky. Vintage fighters and Piper Cubs circle in circus colors or camouflage. Farther west in Minnesota, the birthplace of Lindbergh himself, pontoon planes set down on remote lakes. Beneath the wheat fields and sunflowers of the Dakotas the planted missiles in their silos are supposed to never fly. In Omaha, SAC headquarters hopes to become as sleepy as the hundreds of wind-sock grass runway air parks that dot the fields. Their big bombers once dipped down to the deck and practiced tree-top flying skimming over the grassland and the sand hills. And then I think of Kansas and the factories in Wichita, the production lines of single-family Cessnas, executive jets, turbo-propped puddle jumpers for the growing commuter trade, and even the president's new customized jumbos parked wingtip to wingtip on broiling tarmac. Missouri has its own factories for high-performance military planes, and St. Louis, of course, gave its name to the most famous airplane in the world. At Ida Grove, in Iowa, each summer they refight the Battle of Britain with an armada of quarter-scale radio-controlled model Spitfires and Stukas. How would this fly-in look from the air? Tiny airplanes zipping through the oily smoke of smudge pots set in burning cardboard cities. In Chicago, I also remember gazing up at the life-sized dogfight near the ceiling of the Science and Industry Museum where the real fighters and bombers hung frozen there in pitched battle and served as a model for my own homely dioramas suspended from the ceiling fixtures of my bedroom. There, I strung up plastic models of the *Spirit of St. Louis*, the DC-3, and the P-39 that was built in my hometown during the war. I had pieced them together from kits stamped out in still more factories not far from Chicago. There, too, O'Hare, the world's busiest airport, sits daily inhaling and exhaling the waves of its commercial traffic. Chances are the sophisticated air traveler who sniffs at the Flyover doesn't fly over it at all anymore but descends to one of the several hubs in Chicago, Detroit, Minneapolis, Kansas City, or St. Louis and connects with the remaining spoke of a flight. This down-to-earth, this landlocked Midwest surprises me with its rich connections to flight.

In Hitchcock's *North by Northwest*, the fleeing Cary Grant has been instructed to wait for a contact in the middle of an Indiana cornfield. A bus delivers Grant to the rendezvous site, and it is incredibly desolate, here and there a few stands of corn. Midwesterners know that this can't possibly be Indiana. The horizon is too far away, and the land is (and this is possible) *too* flat. Hitchcock probably filmed it in a California desert, importing the stalks of corn. But the spirit of the place is right. What's on the screen is a massaged landscape that, at first glance, looks natural but on closer inspection yields evidence of complex human tinkering. That replicates the Midwest. It masquerades as wild while it is rich with human drama. There, in the sky, off in the distance, we now see the tiny speck of the crop duster banking, dipping its nose down toward the clueless Grant. The setting of Indiana, of the Midwest, is a crucial part of this famous scene. There is a stark beauty in the minimal props of the still life and the dome of sky that arches over it. The landscape mirrors the frighteningly different world in which the protagonist has been plunged. It is so strange. It has something to do with scale. The sky in the Midwest is just big enough. Even in the most wide-open of places in the Midwest there is still something, far off, bounding it. There are always limits to what you see. No place is completely empty. That copse of trees in the distance, that grassy ridge, that elevator or water tower, they are like islands in an ocean. They turn the space of the sea into a wide-open bay.

When I first moved to Iowa, back to the Midwest from graduate school in Baltimore, a friend from North Dakota gave me a huge poster published by the National Weather Service. It was a cloud chart designed as a spotter's guide, with pictures of three dozen kinds of clouds, all with biological-sounding Latin names and labeled with an alphabet of iconographic symbols. There is *Altocumulus Translucidus Undulatus*, the buttermilk sky, or *Cirrus Uncinus*, the wisp of the mare's tail. My favorite was assigned the code M9, a middle cloud of the ninth kind, called *Altocumulus of a Chaotic Sky*. Working in my office, I'd take a break occasionally and gaze out the window, sometimes using a pair of cheap binoculars to focus on a passing cloud. I kept a log of my sightings in the way birders keep track of their prey.

In the creative writing classes I taught, my students would write that their stories and poems were taking place beneath the Iowa sky, and I would criticize them for not being specific. What is an Iowa sky? I'd ask. What is Iowa for that matter? For them it was so obvious as to be forgotten. They assigned the name to the sky as a shortcut to communicate where they were. I knew the feeling. I too grew up in the Midwest never really thinking about it as a place of any distinction. My home state was just a name. But I had left for a bit and lived under other skies. Returning home, I needed such a chart to help me find where I was. After classes in which I tried to convince my students to sharpen their eyes, I'd rush back up to my own perch and sweep the air for clues. I wanted to see not only what heaven looks like but what that heaven looks down upon.

When I moved to Iowa, I'd get myself invited to my students' farms. On weekends, I'd walk beans or stack hay bales, my ineptitude creating more work for my hosts than I was supposedly relieving them of doing. One fall, I found myself plowing a harvested bean field tucked between the Little Sioux River and the loess bluffs of western Iowa. I was driving a tractor that cost more than the house I had just bought. It had a heated cab and digital readouts of ground speed and exhaust stack temperature, rpms and engine hours. I had tuned in the Sioux City public radio station, where it was pledge week and, honestly, Vivaldi's *Four Seasons* played between pitches for money. The tractor steered hydraulically, humming as its hinged middle made the turns at the end of the field. It was easy to drive. Mr. Brown had showed me, before he turned me loose, the lever used to lower the six-bottom plow and the throttle that moved between the international symbols of fast and slow, cartoon hare and tortoise. The field was huge, and there were no fences. I kept my eye on the distant horizon. I'd glance over my shoulder now and then. There the moldboard plow was turning over the rich black bottom dirt called gumbo. The sky was what my cloud chart calls chaotic, occluded, layered with blankets of thick clouds. It smelled like snow. I crept along listening to the donkeys braying in Vivaldi's Tuscan hills on the radio while all the time I was on farm near Turin, Iowa. When I looked back again at my work, I was astonished to see hundreds of sea birds swooping down out of the gray sky and landing in my wake. Gulls and terns of several makes and markings, more kinds than I could identify since I had grown up so far from any sea. I had been turning over a rich harvest of grubs and worms and the birds on their migration along the ancient flyway of the Missouri River trailed me, circling and diving, as if I were a lobster boat setting pots. But at the time, it seemed miraculous. More birds arrived out of the lowering clouds, settled in the corduroy of furrows as if bobbing on waves. I had drifted along in my little routine, nestled inside the warm cab of a machine so sophisticated it runs itself, when the flocking of birds, newly arrived from the arctic, made clear my actions rippled outward from here, to places around the world and back and forth through time. I was just scratching away in a tiny corner of the earth sending messages I didn't understand to species I never knew existed.

Once again, I was caught up in the midwestern paradox. I felt, simultaneously, my isolation on one of the margins of the world and my connection to what is essential in the scheme of all things.

Putting Myself in My Place

Robert Schuler

> But as I see it, we are today so situated that it is pertinent to ask: What
> for us *is* patient of being "actually loved and known," where for us is
> "this place," where do we seek or find what is "ours," what *is* available,
> what *is* valid as material for our effective signs?
>
> David Jones, preface to *The Anathemata*

Born, raised, and educated in the Bay Area of California, I knew little of
the Midwest. I imagined flat, boring plains and cornfields, the bright lights
and the lust of Chicago's glamorous Rush Street lying somewhere near the
end. Job-searching in Iowa and Illinois, both sprinkled with small liberal
arts colleges, I was not ready for my first February evening in rural northwestern Illinois, broad snowflakes spinning down and round an avenue of
immense black elms, the branches piled high with glistening snow, the
streets impassable, drifted over four feet high with snow. Looming, solid
white, the wooded hills at the northwest edge of town seemed to block the
village off from the rest of the world. Somehow, I was at home. I would
take a job at this college, no matter the salary offer.

Copyright 1995 by Robert Schuler

There's the big advantage of backwardness. By the time the latest ideas reach Chicago they're worn thin and easy to see through. You don't have to bother with them, and it saves trouble.

Saul Bellow, The Dean's December

I want to be backward. I want to live way beyond Chicago, beyond the ring of Taco Bell, the reign of Burger King, *Time*, High-Tech, and the Information Highway.

We have lived in the Midwest now for twenty-seven years. Escaping the clutter, the claustrophobia, the anonymity, the absurd modernity of California, we moved first to the rolling hills of northwestern Illinois and then to wooded western Wisconsin. To be closer to things as they are, should be. To find values closer to bone and soul. In Illinois we bought an old Victorian house, the one I was standing near when I was enchanted by the falling snow. Each day, when I walked out of our bedroom and down the staircase, my eyes were seized by the panorama offered through the two-story-high window: the elm-lined streets of the tiny town, the college campus, and the woods in the distance. I developed a strong affinity with the rhythms of nature. I am still delighted by long, slow snowfalls, the profusion of spring wildflowers, summer rivers, fall's harvests of colors. Hereabouts in Wisconsin the locals can't crush the limestone cliffs and the sharply rising hills into marginal cornfields, or condos, or malls, so we have the pleasure, for the moment, of thick stands of oaks and maples, broad swaths of wildflowers, wild blue phlox, lush pink and red prairie roses, vines full of bright white dewberry and thornberry roses, hills spread with black-eyed Susans, oxeyes, sawtooth sunflowers, lavender sprays of aster, streams and rivers too small to be dammed and damned, charged with wild brook and brown trout, walleyes, white and smallmouth bass. Here I believe I'm in the last temple, a pure place for contemplation. Here I have a chance to be alone, to meditate, to sort myself out, to try to belong to the whole.

Western Wisconsin spins off landscapes and moods familiar to me from my long aesthetic and spiritual affairs with Japanese and Chinese poetry and art:

moon swollen with ice
mist cracking   the hoarse

calls of crows   black capillaries of oaks
wind
twisting
smoke into hair and skin
slow rain unveiling
sand veined with leaves and ashes
bloodroot

The hills seem to have emerged from a Chinese painting. In this area rolling hills, in actuality mounds, fill the eye. From a short distance, they seem to be small mountains, defiant thickets. Often blue mist swaddles them, falls, and hangs between them. In autumn and winter they bristle with black oaks. Downriver many of the wooded mounds are banded at the bottom with mown green meadows, swards. Tiny valleys, swales, open between them. Largely wild land with just a touch of human stewardship and presence. From the tops of the hills I believe I can see the universe in each sacred particular:

smoke
dancing
in the leaves
falling and rising
the crow-
stretched distance

All of my roles and activities are rooted in this land: husband, father, grandfather, friend, woodsman, skier, fisherman, gardener, bird-and-flower lover, university professor, writer, hiker. Minutes from my house, I can ski for fourteen miles past abandoned barns, broken windmills; saw down, log off, and split many winters' worth of windfalls of oaks, maples, and birches; and watch afternoons fill with rose-breasted grosbeaks, eagles, goldfinches, hawks, and blue herons.

Escape? Certainly. But why is the present American socioeconomic world the only one called Reality? Isn't nature equally real? Perhaps more real? Less artificial, distorted? While I am walking by the river my mind often becomes so clear that I can solve or better come to grips with vexing problems that stem from my work and social life.

I love to walk, almost aimlessly, down a trail through the woods or by the Mississippi. In an over-the-shoulder pack, I carry a bird book, a wildflower book, binoculars, snacks, insect repellent, sample bags, a water bottle, pens, a notebook. An afternoon's walk downriver, the river hustling and hissing, might feature hawks whistling out of the woods, a tanager's flaming slash, the breathtaking freshly washed blue of a bluebird, darting wood ducks, pheasants blasting out of the bush, egrets goose-stepping in the springs, a flock of cedar waxwings flitting about the branches of an oak or sumac, herons hunched in ponderous ghost-blue flight.

I cannot tell you how many of my mornings or afternoons have been enriched by the performances of ospreys, eagles, herons, vultures, hawks, and egrets. Last week I turned a bend in the river only to find an osprey hunting. He seemed intent upon exhibiting all of his skills; he glided, soared, and breasted the wind, the undersides of his wings fully spread out against it, then bounced back off of it, hovered, swooped, plunged straight down, disappeared into the river, and bobbed up a few feet downstream, fishless. Most ospreys I've watched are efficient fishermen or fisherwomen, heaving their victims up with their talons, flying smoothly, the fish's head neatly pointed nestwards.

Each October the tundra swans arrive on their way from the Arctic; they spend six weeks to two months feasting on the arrowroot and wild celery that flourish in Rieck's Lake near Alma, Wisconsin. After levering their food loose with their feet and eating it, they spend most of their time floating lazily round the cold waters, but, along about late afternoon, they take a notion to fly. They whistle, hiss, grunt, babble, and run at the water; they bash it with their wings and legs. As they fly overhead, in groups of three or more, their wings sound like rustling silk. When they land, after wheeling over the lake, they form a line, a chain, and splash down, one by one, background snow and ice brocaded black with rich braids of Canada geese.

Bald eagles never seem to be in the same spot or pose. Sometimes they slowly flap or sail near the tops of the five- to seven-story pines or oaks that form walls along the Red Cedar River. Often they circle, higher and higher, overhead. They perch in the shadows of the largest pines, on the branches of oaks, near the bends in the river, near the straights of the river along the open fields. Sometimes I find several of them sitting on an old elm that I have named the Zendo tree, after a Zen meditation hall, because its barkless gray branches, which bend, dangle, shoot, dart, and dip every way imaginable, seem to serve the birds as matchless meditation platforms and because the birds seem to be meditating: they are so dignified, so still, so patient, so aware.

You've got to be ready to look up, down, left, right, every direction, for bright white patches of heads and tails that stand out from the massed green, for the quick streaks of black that mark wings flashing over the treeline, for the rustling in the shadows. The last time I saw the huge she-eagle fly low over the trail on her way back to the eyrie, I thought that her feet, tucked under the tail fan, looked just like our cat Chet's black legs, booted white. Wherever, whenever I see an eagle, and usually I see at least one a day, I hold my breath. I am in awe; they are so stately, so dominant in the land-scape.

One day, after searching for many hours, I finally spotted an eagle deep in the shadows of a pine high over the opposite bank. Fixed in my binoculars, he swelled forth, his proud, shaggy white head, his bright eyes, the golden hooked beak, talons clasped round a bare elm branch, white tail feathers pointed down. I watched him turn his head slowly back and forth to command all avenues up- and downriver. Suddenly he swooped down (large eagles and turkey vultures seem to fall from their pedestals directly into flight) and flew upstream, disappearing into a distant patch of oaks. I walked back upstream, hoping that I would see him again, although such is almost never the case. But there he was, poised on a bare oak branch high over the river, swiveling his head slowly back and forth. When he turned in my direction, he swooped off again. I walked about a hundred yards up-stream. There he was again, on top of a leafless elm, staring at me. This time I took off first, on a whim. He appeared to follow me, landing in a rusty pine directly across from a small clearing I had just entered. Visual hopscotch ensued for more than an hour. Through the trees I often saw his broad wings flap and soar just above the water. We met a dozen times. Who was following whom?

This fall I finally saw something I have always wished to see: the courtship behavior of eagles. At Rieck's Lake, a prime spot for watching just about every kind of duck as well as Canada geese and eagles and tundra swans, two eagles circled high above the water. They began to dive playfully at one another, to chase one another to and fro. Suddenly, they grasped one another's talons, hand in hand, so to speak, and cartwheeled down the sky, broad wing over wing, body over body. It seemed that they would crash into the trees below, but they broke away just in time and gracefully resumed their airborne dance.

One of my favorite places to visit is County Road Q, for the broad fields and hills that it cuts and rolls through are fine hunting spots for eagles and hawks. In winter I love to watch the hawks swoop down, their tail fans staining the snow rose-tan. In summer the eagles slowly ride the warm winds up and up until they disappear, leaving the steaming afternoons graceless.

Another spot I'm fond of, an unlikely one at that, is Wilson Creek, which feeds into the Red Cedar. For two miles Wilson runs just below Highway 25, the main street of Menomonie, a busy little town of just over 13,000 souls. You can canoe down the Wilson and occasionally hear and see rather thick truck and automobile traffic above. But this "in-town" section of the Wilson smacks of wilderness. The ragged, forgotten fields of farms spill toward the creek. Beavers are constantly at work, unconcerned with canoeists who practically brush shoulders with them. A sandhill crane rackets out of a patch of reeds, as we paddle up the creek, admiring the cracked and twisted blocks of towerlike palisades. Pines sprout trunk-thick roots that snake waterwards. Leaves float burgundy, gold, chablis. Out of a pale willow two hawks leap (this is the closest I've ever been to a raptor) and sail round the stream bend.

As I walk, I wonder whether I am opening myself up enough to the world, whether I am honestly developing a "fresh perspective" toward the birds, flowers, trees, angles of the sun, depths of shadows. I tell myself and others that I am looking for eagles, but I am simply trying to keep my senses open and my mind still. Looking for eagles is a suitable motive because eagles are so very often difficult to see. In any case, I am training myself to be surprised, to be open-minded and openmouthed. I am also poised to begin writing.

And there's almost always the delight of the unexpected: columns of mist clinging to the wooded bluffs above the Mississippi; a pileated (woody) woodpecker who appears every February afternoon just about five on top of a sumac tree at the same bend in the cross-country skiing trail next to the river; rainbows glistening in the mist of waterfall ravines; cardinals flaring past snowbanks; a pure white star engraved upon the pink, fluted blossoms of the vines of the hedge bindweed; mounds of bristling black oaks imprisoning red bands of sunfall; instead of the blue heron you expect to find hunching in your binoculars, a fawn bouncing into the shadows of a feeder spring; dozens of turkey vultures soaring gracefully, slightly tilting and rocking their wings, far overhead; the lavender sparks of New England asters scattered generously against the fading September woods; bumblebees tumbling round the soft cones of sweet white clover; the unearthly cyan blue of an Indigo bunting; the hoarse squawk of an alarmed heron; a doe and her fawn, sun crinkling in buckskin, as they swallow your cherry-red asiatic lilies; the tall bellflower; the bronzed smallmouth bass. There are always other genii to meet.

Even what's most expected—the rich colors of autumn leaves, a display that draws people here from Chicago and from all over the Midwest—entrances. Against cool blue air streaked with cream or pewter sky or black mist, the rich swatches of the willows, maples, birches, sumac, and oak: pale grasshopper green, pale yellow and gold, burnt orange, chocolate, burnt umber, ocher, dark apple red, scarlet, amber, cherry, blaze rose, and rust red.

Sometimes I see the land in a series of layers:

trail, early May

the hazy iron-gray
layered mazes of the woods and hills
streaked white with birch trunks
stained rose with the gathered buds of maples
tall grass fallen all along the ditches

filled with swamp buttercup
green hills sprinkled
pink with spring
beauties   white with bloodroot
deep in the back   high on the hillsides
under jade green screens of pines
between the boulders
thousands of patches of snow
trillium

Nature is a pure gift, a blessing. It is constantly giving: air, food, water, shelter, clothing, beauty, an *embarras de richesses*. It should be the cynosure of our thanksgiving, admiration, and awe. I believe it is the primary cause of the experience of the holy, for it constantly presents us with forces that humans realize they cannot create and cannot wholly control (alas, humans can easily destroy nature, and we continue to eliminate more than 300,000 acres of essential wetlands each year). In the heart of nature humans should realize that they are no more than a part of the whole, that they have evolved through time within ecosystems that have also evolved and have given unto them by supporting them (humans have seldom, save perhaps in the National Parks, supported nature; they must learn to do so). We should be humble in the presence of nature. When I am, I realize, as did Walt Whitman, that what I see, what I hear, and what I feel are "miracles."

This is a place, lost, lonely in the howl of summer winds and rains and the seamless mists and blizzards, a point without light, where I am an ear listening to what's beyond. This is a place where I feel worthy of becoming a soul:

these lovely hours spent
listening to rain
slow rain
Schumann's manic piano
and the circling
violins of Brahms

Above all, there is the peace of space. The land creates most of my writing. It's a continual inspiration. A "sense of place," in reality, a love for the animals, woods, flowers, rivers, hills, is absolutely necessary for my writing, my life. The structures of man that incessantly cut away have become anathema to me.

Our senses of time and mission are flawed. We must be practical. We must be busy; we must accomplish something. Why not spend more time in re-creation and celebration? In "There Was a Child Went Forth," Walt Whitman, in still another almost breathless catalogue, tells of all the lives that have entered and shaped his life, of all of the flowers, birds, animals, and people that have contributed their beauty and their energy to the growth of his soul. I am much like the child at the end of the poem, feeling the edges of the world touch him, ready to explore, anxious to meet the next other, the next unexpected moment. What a privilege and blessing it is to allow the lives of nature to enter ours. To watch and listen to myriad others. To silence the raucous, chattering monkey voice of the ego. To ponder, meditate the powers and purposes of the life-force and its minions. To be one wandering among the many spirits that inhabit this world. To be startled, to see the burning bush, the illuminating vision, to receive, with humility, grace.

I feel blessed to live in a house within and under the quivering shadows of red oak, white oak, and maple woods that shelter several wildflower gardens and provide food for owls, woodpeckers, grouse, squirrels, and deer. Last year a glowering great horned owl took up a two-week perch in our backyard. Hawks often sail through, eagles over. Not long ago our muddy backyard was stained rose by swarming flocks of finches.

> Good Lord how petty we've become
> so quick
> to bitch
> we ignore all of this
> good luck
> daylilies colored by Bonnard
> the bright-
> blue swirling jays
> the fuchsia blurs of hummingbirds

Working out of doors brings me closely in touch with the rhythms of nature. I love the demanding physical labor of felling a dead or dying tree with a chain saw, sawing the trunk and large branches into rounds, and splitting them into firewood. When splitting a piece of hardwood, I can often feel the shock of the impact of the woodmaul against the round rippling down my arms, my back, my legs.

splitting wood

rounds of oak trunks   bark and bands of warped white
woodflesh bound to ice
sun bouncing down black mazes of branches
last year's leaves pasted to ground   pale as sand
the body begins again
axe arc   hot in the wrist   the pounding wind   the heart

Often I dig new garden beds in the areas of my lot left barren by the fall of a granddaddy oak or maple. In such gardens I plant, in addition to tulips, daffodils, iris, daylilies, and asiatic lilies, wildflowers such as harebells, dutchman's-breeches, bloodroot, spring beauties, starflowers, Canada anemone, violets, swamp buttercup, trillium, wild pink and white roses, and wild geraniums. June evenings the wild blue phlox seems to float all over the top of the garden, staining the other flowers, the grass, even the shadows, silver-blue.

I suppose I cannot get enough beauty. I relish the loveliness of each flower in my garden, like the black speckled throat of the dewberry rose, the wildflowers and trees on the trails near the Red Cedar and the Mississippi, the grace and power of the birds I quest after.

Fishing is still another way I enter nature. Suffice it to say that fishing hones one's ability to concentrate and meditate; thus, while focusing on the fly, the jig, the plug as it is tugged softly or harshly downstream, you see water pouring over the falls to your right, a heron thudding his wings upstream, a deer wading across the river through the shallows you thought to be depths from a distance, a patch of woodland sunflowers bouncing in the wind. And there is the electric connection that can be fashioned, for moments, between your life and the life of the other:

```
bone-damp     raindawn
wandering pool to blank pool
until the shock of a strike
and I ride the rainbow
down the singing line
```

I realize that I have been strongly influenced by those who have gone
before me: William Blake, the poets of the T'ang Dynasty, Robinson Jeffers, Gary Snyder, Aldo Leopold, William Faulkner (especially in *The Bear*),
Emily Dickinson. My original responses to nature have been sharpened and
enhanced by so many writers and naturalists. They have taught me to respect, to see, to enjoy nature. They were generous. I should like to be generous in turn.

Sometimes the poem is naught but an attempt to register an experience,
a perception. Some years back I skied nearly every day past a gorgeous pair
of trumpeter swans:

```
skiing along the river
through the misty float of snow
past swans
```

Once I saw scarlet tanagers, Baltimore orioles and goldfinches circling,
endlessly it seemed, a cherry tree that had just blossomed. I titled the piece
"This Tree of Lights," alluding to all of the trees that have seemed to contain the light of sacred truth, the aura, illumination, perhaps the sparks of
the Kabbala.

```
glare-yellow     fire-orange     scarlet
flares
goldfinches     Baltimore orioles     tanagers
whirling round
foaming
fountains of cherry blossoms
```

In late fall, just before the first snowfall, and in late winter and early
spring, before, during, and after thaw, the land seems to be barren, feature-
less, bleak, but these are the *très riches heures* of swans, eagles, hawks, and,

especially, Canada geese, their apparently distraught moans, the black arrowheads of their migrating flights cutting the hoary air south or north.

Snow re-creates place, shrinks it, brings it closer, silences it. A thick snowfall quickly turns a pine copse into a white wall, or a series of white castles. A field of tall brown grass bends down dappled white. Woods and hills seam together. Heaven spills into earth.

Extremes of temperature do not bother me. I ski in the midst of biting winds. Parts of my face may sting, but the rest of my body will be warm with sweat. On a long summer walk, furnace heat wilting the woodland sunflowers, blazing stars, bergamot, and white hemlock, I delight in the exercise, the bath of sweat, a cardinal flaring downwind, an upside-down flicker attacking a red oak, a deer, hoarse, out of breath, bounding out of the bush just in front of me. Here is a poem for July First:

> sun catches
> buckskin in the wings
> and tails of two hawks sailing
> over a streambank
> sewn quilt-thick with black-eyed
> golden Susans

The world of nature is the richest poem I know.

Literature has awakened and enhanced my sense of nature. Great works of art still serve as strong sources of inspiration for me. Many midwestern writers have etched unforgettably strong lines in my life, but the two most powerful, most resonant voices, will always be those of Willa Cather and Thomas McGrath. Cather, especially in *My Ántonia*, repeatedly evokes the mystical beauty and power of nature. I will always remember Jim in his grandmother's garden, recently carved out of the wilderness of the prairies, experiencing union with nature, the godhead:

> I was something that lay under the sun and felt it, like the pumpkins, and I
> did not want to be anything more. I was entirely happy. Perhaps we feel
> like that when we die and become a part of something entire, whether it
> is sun or air, or goodness and knowledge. At any rate, that is happiness; to
> be dissolved into something complete and great.

And Jim watching the high red grass sway like a sea in the wind. Jim and Ántonia in the midst of a rainstorm: "The thunder was loud and metallic, like the rattle of sheet iron, and the lightning broke in great zigzags across the heavens, making everything stand out and come closer to us for a moment." The trail of sunflowers: "a gold ribbon across the prairie." The magic plow etched into the sun. I love Cather's accuracy and clarity as well as her reverence for the commonplace features in nature.

Thomas McGrath has rendered the particulars of the midwestern landscape in rhythms that rise out of and sail beyond the English lyrical tradition. In *Letter to an Imaginary Friend*, we witness not only the mastery of assonance, alliteration, consonance, and the long line, but also the full, precise revelation of place. McGrath makes us see the trees and the tiny wildflowers that provide idiosyncratic characteristics to place, and he makes us hear the sounds and distinctive movements of the animals, our fellow inhabitants. In McGrath's work, as I have written elsewhere, "place has been sharply visualized, sharply and hauntingly sounded, felt, the reader caught in the round dance, the round song."

Cather and McGrath always make me realize how fortunate I am—we are—to have much of the old world still in place. No, I could not live, I could not teach, without a true place.

Occasionally, I have the strong fear that I must see things today, for they will be gone tomorrow. The pair of trumpeter swans was murdered by a drunken hunter some years ago. Swans are not to be found on any stretch of the river that runs through town. Every year people shoot at tundra swans, claiming they "seemed to be snow geese." This spring just north of here seventeen bald eagles died horrible deaths from toxic chemicals maliciously implanted in a dead animal's body. Local fishermen keep too many fish, and I have seen many healthy patches of woods and wildflowers disappear overnight. Several years ago the loveliest grove of elms in town gave way, the afternoon droning with chain saws, to a squat gray cement-block of a building that houses Domino's Pizza. They are bulldozing a new housing development on the edges of Wilson Creek. Much of the topsoil in the Midwest spins aimlessly in the waves of the Atlantic Ocean. A rose isn't always a rose. Perhaps the tree of lights will appear around the next corner and never appear again. I would experience a long and dark night of the soul. I pray that these places will be here for my grandchildren. Last fall my oldest grandson saw his first hawk, which he greeted with a broad smile and a loud, exuberant "Hi!" I worship nature for her manifold blessings and offer the deepest thanksgiving for them.

The Roosting Tree

Mary Swander

How do they find their way? By the stars? Wherever I've gone, wherever I've lived, I've looked for them—the monarchs, those majestic gold-and-black butterflies that dip and dive over milkweed plants and alight on garden stakes, their wings spreading in the sun. In their transience, they are one of the most anchoring images of my present life in Fairview School. Through the stages of their metamorphosis, they are one of my most vivid memories from my first childhood home.

In Manning, a tiny town in western Iowa, thousands of monarchs gathered every year in the fall. For one night they landed in the silver maple tree right outside my bedroom window in our old white house. Their legs clinging to the sappy branches, their wings extended, they became a huge ball of orange fire descending upon the maple. With their wings folded in at sunset, they mimicked the tree's leaves, their bodies swinging and swaying in the cool autumn breeze that blew in from the north over the rustling

"The Roosting Tree," from *Out of this World* by Mary Swander. Copyright 1995 by Mary Swander. Reprinted by permission of Viking Penguin, a division of Penguin Books USA Inc.

and browning cornfields. In the morning, their wings opening again, expanding, they launched back into the air and drifted south.

In the 1950s, we knew where the butterflies summered, but where they wintered was still a mystery. The western monarch's overwintering site had long been known—a grove of pine trees, oddly enough, near a motel in Monterey, California. But the eastern monarch's route had never been quite determined, and their overwintering site in the mountains about one hundred miles north of Mexico City wouldn't be discovered until 1974. When butterflies took off on those fall mornings, I watched them float away toward some unknown destination. Where were they going? How did they know when to leave? How did their offspring, several generations later, know how to retrace the same route, landing in the very same tree year after year?

As the monarchs came and went throughout my childhood, so have they followed me through my adult life. Like most from my generation of baby boomers, I've moved around a lot—probably twenty times in the same number of years. One year I moved six times, and since then, still have things—photograph books and mementos—that have never been taken out of boxes. They've sat in attics, packed and ready to go at the slightest warning. I learned to pride myself on how easily I could make moves, keeping a wad of money stashed away just for damage deposits and first-month's rent checks. I thinned out my wardrobe and winnowed out my furniture to light items I could lift myself and preferably fold up and put in the trunk of my car. I got to know two movers, swarthy, muscular men who looked like pirates in their sleeveless T-shirts with tattoos engraved on their bulging biceps. They became experts at piling up four or five boxes of my books at once on their backs and carrying them down three flights of stairs.

"See you again next year," the pirates said when I paid them at the end of the day.

Moving became an avocation. Routinely, I read the rental ads and kept my eyes trained for signs posted on lawns and in windows. I listened for friends who were leaving town and asked about their apartments. I helped other people find places to live, matching landowner with lessee, renter with subletter. I moved unnecessarily. I moved just to be three blocks closer to the commuter train or to have a bank of windows with a southern exposure.

Throughout my teenage years, I'd lain awake at night and dreamed of moving. This wasn't the usual adolescent desire to mature and leave the nest, but a deeper, more shame-ridden kind of longing. This was a longing intrinsic to the small towns and moderate-size cities of the Midwest. This was Willa Cather leaving Red Cloud, Nebraska, on the hot, dusty train for Pittsburgh. This was F. Scott Fitzgerald bidding good-bye to St. Paul, Minnesota, Hemingway to Oak Park, Illinois.

"I've got to get out of this dump," I told myself when I left Iowa for college in Washington, D.C., and rejoiced in my good fortune to be moving away from a place where the world perceived its people to be as flat and boring as its landscape. I was never coming back. No, I would never return. The thought made me giddy. The thought made me panic. Nothing would ever be familiar again, but oh well, there was nothing for me back *there*.

"There's no there there," Gertrude Stein said of her home in Oakland, California, as she glanced back across the ocean from her domicile-in-exile outside Paris. Her remark became emblematic for me as I slid through my early twenties, my nuclear family dispersed or dead. There was no there there. There was no one home there. There was no home to go home to.

There was still a house. That huge, rambling childhood house. It stood in the center of town, on the corner of April and First Streets. Once, it had been the banker's home, and ever since had been known as the old Dutton place. At the turn of the century, the Dutton place was the kind of house the Midwest is made of, a house in a town with twenty trains a day whizzing in and out and a burgeoning farm economy, a house that dripped of immigrant optimism and faith in life in the New World. Its widow's walk, its gingerbread porch railings, its stained-glass windows, its gazebo and the circular drive where the Dutton daughter rode her pony round and round, all spoke of an affluence that the rest of the townspeople at once grumbled about and aspired to.

By the 1930s, the Dutton place stood empty, the wind blowing through the broken windows, the Virginia creeper vines pushing in through the holes in the glass. The Depression had a leveling effect on small-town life, and most of these fine old houses had been either chopped up into rooming houses or converted to funeral homes. My grandparents bought the ailing old Dutton place for $1,000, having moved back to my grandmother's hometown to live out their final years. They went about their business in the downstairs while a succession of schoolteachers and laborers took up residence above, the smell of a boarder's soup warming on a hot plate wafting through the air in the early evening, the sounds of snoring echoing down the stairway at night.

In 1950, my mother made the migration home to Iowa from Chicago, pregnant and with two small boys and a husband whose Illinois naval reserve unit was about to be called up for the Korean war. The change of residence was to be a temporary thing, until I was born and the war was over. The schoolteachers were moved out and our little family in, the hot plates replaced by a full-size stove and refrigerator. But then the years stretched out, and even when we did move across the state ten years later to Davenport, I returned to the old Dutton place every summer to live with my grandmother. It was there, and only there that ever seemed like home.

In my mid-twenties I inherited the old Dutton place and went back for a summer to clean it out of four generations' worth of accumulations. I worked alone, fixing the house up for sale, the heat one hundred degrees in the attic, where piles of boxes held piles of other boxes: my great-grandmother's tea tin she brought from Ireland, my grandmother's crate of crucifixes she'd saved from the coffins of twenty-five family members she'd buried, my mother's jewelry box with the locket she'd worn and nervously put in her mouth, the teeth marks still indented in the gold-plated metal.

Downstairs, one generation's stuff bled into another, the result of a Depression mentality that stuck with us for decades. In our household, money was saved by saving things, recycling and putting even the smallest scrap of scratch paper to good use. Take my grandfather's equipment, for example. Just before I was born, my grandfather died and left his office full of old books, glass vials, and torturous-looking stainless-steel instruments. My family quickly utilized these belongings in its own mundane way, and I arrived into a world of medical metaphor. I grew up watching my mother pluck her eyebrows by staring into my grandfather's magnifying mirror, which he wore clamped around his head for eye, ear, nose, and throat exams. My brother clipped the dog's fur with a pair of old surgical scissors, and I used surgical tweezers to spread the wings of the mounted butterflies in my collection. My grandmother threw a tablecloth over my grandfather's examining table and shoved it into her breakfast nook. Every morning I drank my juice and ate my toast bumping into stirrups.

Flashlight in hand, that hot summer I sifted, sorted, and stacked things in piles in the dark reaches of that attic and thought about home. What was it? A geographical location? A physical structure? A house? A teepee, igloo, or boat? A bunch of junk handed down from one generation to the next? No, no, I told myself, it's the people who inhabit that structure. But as I moved downstairs to scrub out the kitchen sink, I realized even more than ever before that those people were gone and still I felt that this house—now almost empty of furniture and artifacts, the rooms ghostly with echoes—still felt like home.

Memories, then, I told myself, taking down the heavy draperies in the living room that Olga had made, her gray hair bent over her sewing machine. A home is not so much the people as the memories of the people who inhabited it. I remembered Olga on a stepladder, slipping the draperies over their three-pronged hooks, my mother feeding the material up to her, and when they were finished, the two of them sitting at the kitchen table for coffee and doughnuts, Olga's full lips parting in laughter when our little wire-hair fox terrier sat up on her haunches, begging for a bit of the pastry.

"*Ach*," Olga said, slipping the dog a few crumbs, "who can resist that?"

Recollections, who can resist those? I asked myself. Recollections are what's important, I said, dragging furniture, books, and kitchen wares out on the street for an auction, these last items too big, heavy, or insignificant for me to carry around for the rest of my life. Watching buyers load up a box of old canning jars on their pickup truck, I realized I was sending on memories, that another family would incorporate these items into their lives, and like a quilt made of scraps of clothes, these objects would have another life, another layer of reminiscence. I have my memories, I told myself repeatedly when the For Sale sign went up in front of the old Dutton place. I can't hold on to the house anymore, but my internal picture of it is still intact.

The house was sold right after Labor Day. I sat down on the front steps and wept, but then felt a strange presence surrounding me. I raised my head out of my lap to see one monarch butterfly, then another glide in over the lawn and alight on the silver maple. They were back, the monarchs on the same tree, making their migration. Scientists have speculated that the butterflies may find their way to the same roosting trees through the use of pheromones, or hormonal scent markings, not sensed by the human nose but strong enough to attract insects over a hundred miles away. Human behavior is influenced by pheromones too. On a subtle yet powerful level, our own smells attract the opposite sex in a much more dramatic way than any perfume. Pheromones keep us hormonally attuned, even in same-gender situations. Women living in close proximity, as in college dorms, tend to synchronize their menstrual periods through pheromones.

Perhaps my attraction for the Dutton place went beyond the reach of happy childhood memories, of family solidarity, to a deeper, intangible bond. Twenty years and twenty living spaces later, that's the home of my dreams, the bedroom that brings me safety and refuge in my happy reveries, the driveway I'm trying to reach over and over again in my nightmares. My peers, fellow graduates of the baby-boom-moving-school, suggest that a sense of home has nothing to do with actual geography or physical space, that home is something internal, spiritual, what you carry around inside you.

This is certainly a mobile concept, and much more uplifting than Frost's home-is-the-place-where-when-you-have-to-go-there-they-have-to-take-you-in mode of thinking. But most of my friends, especially those in academia or the corporate business world, plunk themselves down in a locale or a house for which they have no affinity. Many of them live for five to fifteen years in a spot that does not tug at their psyche or soul. They aren't interested in the history of the place, nor the evolution of its landscape and environment. Instead, they hope nearby are good restaurants and schools, and a cheap fitness club. No, as much as I like the ephemeral no-

tion of home, I like exploring the opposite idea, that home may be an almost physiological tug toward a concrete physical place.

After I sold the old Dutton place, I went back to Chicago, lived there for
three years, and thought of the Zen story of the two men who were moving
to the same new town and feeling a lot of anxiety about the transition.
They both went to the Zen master and asked him if their new town would
be a good place in which to live.

"How did you like your last home?" the master asked the first man.

"Oh, I loved it. It was wonderful," the man said.

"You'll like your new town very much," the master said, then turned to
the second man, asking him the same question.

"I hated that place," the second man said. "It was a horrible town."

"Then you'll be very unhappy in your new home," the master said.

Perhaps it was my karma, then, not to fall in love with Chicago. I didn't
dislike it. I loved riding the el downtown on Friday nights to attend the
Chicago Symphony or a poetry reading at the Museum of Contemporary
Art, grabbing a quick meal first at Berghoff's, the waiters whisking the
plates and silverware on and off the white tablecloths with enormous speed
and efficiency. I loved walking along the lake at dusk, the water a deep tur-
quoise, rolling out toward the horizon. I loved clicking on my radio to the
Studs Terkel show every morning, his gravelly voice interviewing everyone
from Itzhak Perlman to the national champion Irish fiddle player. But when
my Chicago job began to implode, I knew the city was not the kind of
place I was tuned into enough to stay and settle for good. Quite surprisingly, I found myself thinking about moving back to Iowa, not to
Manning—that would be just too isolated and cut off—but to Iowa City, a
larger, university town that had made cameo appearances in my life since I
was very small.

The money from the sale of the old Dutton place was enough for a down
payment on Ida's place, an old five-room house in Iowa City built about at
the turn of the century. The house stood in a humble neighborhood of very
old and very young homeowners—widows and retired laborers, singles and
newlyweds in their early thirties buying "fixer-uppers." Just on the other

side of the tracks, a block outside of the official inner ring of student ghetto housing and the roundhouse of the Northwestern railroad, the neighborhood withstood the head-splitting midnight bangings of the coupling cars, tolerable only to the poor who could find no escape, the deaf, and those still too engrossed in the newness of their own couplings to care.

Ida's place was a story and a half, the two tandem bedrooms upstairs squatting squarely above the living and dining room below. A great old brick chimney ran up through the center of the home, the plates over the opening for the wood stove pipes still there, unpainted, not plastered or papered over, their pastoral winter scenes complete with sleighs and red-cheeked children. The dwelling had once been on the outskirts of the city, a small farmhouse on the edge, surrounded by open prairie. Until the 1950s, this was still mostly the case, until lots were subdivided and most of the other houses in the neighborhood moved in. Outside, its large yard, almost a quarter acre, with its fruit trees and garden space, its grapevines, lilac hedges, and raspberry canes, was more alluring than the home itself, the tin roof rusting, the old fishscale shingles covered by asbestos ones.

Ida's had been standing empty for three years when I bought it, the windows cracked and vandalized, the Virginia creeper vines winding their way inside. Like my grandparents, I saw a bargain, and the price tag for this house included everything that was in it, the complete belongings of the ninety-year-old woman who had lived there for twenty years. The day I got the keys, the contents of the place were exactly the same as the day Ida left, carried out on a stretcher by paramedics and rushed to the hospital after a stroke. Her coffee cup was still in the sink, her apron slung over the kitchen chair, a load of laundry strung on a rope in the basement to dry.

Her son and daughter, in their seventies with health problems of their own, did not have the energy or sentiment to go through the mother's belongings. Even with a housing shortage in the city, the place did not sell.

"I'd show the house," the real-estate agent said, nudging me to sign my name on the final papers, "and unlike you, people just couldn't see beyond the mess."

Yes, I knew mess, and had to mess with the mess before I could move in my collapsible furniture and boxes of books. First, I let the family come and take whatever they wanted. They carted off the photographs, the silver, china, and an old Victrola, then on my first day of ownership, I hired a dump truck and literally scooped and carried out eight loads of junk. Anything that wasn't worth anything went: newspapers and magazines, old industrial-size cans full of lard, mattresses, canning jars full of homemade grape juice, a thin layer of botulism and mold swimming along the top. I pulled up the tattered rugs and down the heavy draperies. I washed the windows and scrubbed the floors, disinfected the bathtub.

Underneath the refuse were some nice antiques—a caned rocking chair, a library table, and a bureau—and underneath the *Organic Gardening* magazines stuffed in the drawers of the bureau unfolded Ida's life. From her scrapbooks and artifacts, I pieced together her history, how she'd grown up on a farm near Iowa City, and been courted from Kalona, fifteen miles away, mostly through penny postcards in the mail.

March 20, 1908

Dear Ida,

Just to let you know that I made it home from the dance okay. Didn't get back until 2 a.m., though, with the horse pulling as hard as she could through the snow. I hope to be back in town near Easter.
Until then,
Ed

I found Ed's gun and spurs from the Spanish-American War, Ida's wedding dress, and their son's baptismal gown. I followed her children through their schooling and report cards. I found Ida and Ed's fiftieth anniversary card. Different plates and mugs with insignia from various dorms across campus traced her career as a cook for the university. Everything was marked and labeled in a wobbly scrawl. *This is the shirt Ed wore when he took his last breath. This is the pillow where Ed laid his head when he took his last breath. This is the rag I used to wipe Ed's brow when he laid his head on the pillow to take his last breath.*

This plain country woman who lived a simple life in a simple house was very emotional and sentimental. Perhaps most moving of all were the numerals she had saved from the other houses she'd lived in during her adult life. Wrapped in a silk handkerchief, they fell out into my hand, the numbers and little pieces of paper providing the street addresses: *2308 Muscatine Ave.* and *109 Governor.* In her scrapbooks and letters, she constantly navigated by her sense of place. *He gave me this in the Muscatine house,* she scrawled under an old Valentine from Ed, and *That was in the Governor house,* she added under their daughter's birth announcement.

Ida's identity with place pervaded the house. As I sorted through her belongings, I felt like an intruder. And I was. Ida, you see, was still alive! A massive stroke was not enough to fell this strong woman, just enough to land her in a nursing home for the rest of her days.

"Whatever you do, don't sell my house!" she'd told her son as soon as she moved to the long-term county care facility. "I'm going home."

"Don't worry, Mother. Your house'll be there for you," her son said, and a week later the For Sale sign went up in the yard.

For five more years, after I bought her home, Ida hung on, pushing a hundred before she finally died in the nursing home, her son having passed away three years before her. During that time, not a day went by when I didn't think of her, didn't make some psychic space for her, didn't run into some little reminder of the life that had inhabited that home before me. Her home was still there for her, and she was there for me—both with curses and blessings. Through the quirks of her house, I began to slip inside the workings of her mind.

One day, with the robins whistling in the mulberry tree, I dragged the stepladder outside to remove the storm windows, only to find them nailed onto the house. Lily, the eighty-year-old neighbor woman who pushed her push lawn mower ten blocks to the shop every spring to have the blades sharpened, told me that in Ida's last years in the house, she had gotten fearful that someone was going to break in. Winter and summer, she kept the storms on, long twopenny nails securing them to the window frames. I swore at her that day when I had to climb onto the roof with a crowbar, a rope tied around my waist for safety, to pry loose the windows from the second story.

I praised her, though, when I glanced down at the flower bed below:

there were her plantings, which heralded the beginning of spring—cro-cuses, tulips, and the beautiful white pasqueflower. Inside, Ida's whole household attested to the fact that her real focus was outside. Her gardening gloves, her trowel, and muddy black rubbers that fit snugly over her oxfords rested on the basement steps right next to the back door. In the cellar, she'd set up a summer kitchen, complete with an old cookstove, a huge pressure cooker on the burner, and dozens of blue Mason jars, some with dates stretching back before the Civil War.

Without a window that would open, the hot, steaming water of August canning season would have made the upstairs kitchen unbearable, but there was something hidden, and sacred, about this catacomb operation that appealed to the primitive, private side of myself. Here was energy at the very core, the very bottom of things—fuel and food. Here was a place of hibernation, of preservation, the long winter wait before renewal. Eleven short steps up, the yard opened into the rough terrain of Ida's former vegetable plot, the grass grown over the rows. I reopened her plot and began the first garden of my adult life there.

Following the chronology of her scrapbooks, I watched Ida's adult life yield back to childhood. Her early books contained themes she had written in a one-room school, describing the May baskets she'd filled with wild-flowers from the fields and groves around her house. The margins of the yellowed paper were covered with drawings of bluebells, spring beauties, and pasqueflowers, large bold butterflies resting on the petals. Then, in her last years, her books again returned to the simplicity of a mind delighted by nature. Drawings and photographs of birds, chipmunks, and deer clipped from newspapers and church bulletins were pasted on her black pages. A large color shot of a monarch butterfly drifting above a milkweed plant graced the last page of the last book.

One evening that first fall, the canning jars full of beans and tomatoes neatly arranged on the cellar shelves, I stepped out onto the front porch to rest in a lawn chair, and spotted monarchs gliding over the garden, their wings folding and unfolding like the pages of Ida's scrapbooks. First there were twenty butterflies, then thirty. They circled and landed on flowers, shrubs, and trees until they settled at last on the low-hanging limbs of Lily's sugar maple, its leaves just beginning to turn a bright orange, one shade lighter than the monarch's wings. The butterflies' numbers weren't enough to transform the sugar maple into the roosting tree of my youth, but they did make me feel that I had something right. I'd found a spot along my route where all the conditions were perfect for me to land and thrive—for at least another year.

I never met Ida, never went to visit her in the nursing home, as many friends and acquaintances had urged me to do. I never knew if she'd ever been told that her house had been sold and I preferred to leave her memories intact. I preferred not to interfere with that pull she felt toward home, and the hope that she would eventually migrate back there again.

"Don't you dare sell my house." I heard her voice in the attic, in the cellar, in the pear tree outside. It was as if her words were pheromone molecules, markings she'd left on the place. She'd lived in that house twenty years. Why couldn't that be her roost for five more years in her mind?

The couple that had lived in the house before Ida had occupied the place for some fifty years, but never felt the same bond. Instead, they were pulled back to their ancestral home.

"You've never heard the story of Mr. and Mrs. Story?" Lily said to me one day over coffee and doughnuts. "They were from Ireland, but lived here all these years, planted these fruit trees, tilled the first garden spot. Then he decided he wanted to go back home to die. They left. Just like that. Sold the house to Ida. He wasn't even sick, but when they got to Ireland, he died. Happy, I guess."

Miriam Rothschild, a renowned self-taught naturalist and researcher on butterflies and moths, was never happy unless she was living in a home outside the city. "All the big dramas happen in the country," she contended. Her work showed how the monarch butterfly uses plant toxins as a defense mechanism. By storing within itself poisons drawn from the milkweed plant—poisons to which the monarch has evolved an immunity—the butterfly makes itself quite unpalatable to birds and spiders.

The circumstances surrounding my illness pushed me out of Ida's house and along another migratory route. By sheer fluke, several years later, I found Fairview School, and the minute I peeked in the door and saw the view of the rolling hills open up outside the bank of the six-foot-tall windows, I was certain that I could be happy to make my home there. By coming to a spot in the middle of the Amish community, isolated and as far away as one can get in this society from the reaches of the world, I knew I'd find sanctuary, if not immunity, from the birds and spiders of my life that sought to consume me.

Fairview School was still serving the area until 1985. The student population was about ninety percent Amish, although some neighborhood English did attend, blending right into the fabric of the whole. A certified teacher taught classes with twenty-five to thirty students, or "scholars," squeezed into the 25-by-25 space at any given time. Then, in the mid-eighties, the students were moved into town and the doors of Fairview School were closed, the desks, books, blackboards, and even the bell tower put up for sale at auction.

When I bought the place, the school had—what else?—been standing empty for three years, the farmer owner thinking he would use the structure for haying his cattle. "I thought I might build a loft and manger in here, open the doors, and let the critters roam through," he told me. "Then I said, no, I'd try to put it up for sale first."

When I roamed through, instead of holding a herd of Herefords, the place was filled with dust, cobwebs, and mice. The walls were painted hospital green, and what plumbing there was creaked, spit, and leaked, the well filling up with water after every snowmelt. I swept and scrubbed and lived there for six weeks before renovation began, camping out on the floor in my sleeping bag, mouse traps clicking their way into the night like castanets. I had no phone, no oven, no refrigerator. I kept my food cold by placing it in a box outside. I cooked soups and stews and heated water on top of the wood stove.

I had a table, a chair, and a stool, my clothes hanging on a hook on the back of the door. I used the phone next door in the Amish phone booth, and drove into town and took a shower at the gym. Life was pared down about as far as I'd ever known, and once or twice, when a couple of friends stopped in to visit, their eyes widened in disbelief. But I simply pulled a couple of mugs out of the "library" cabinet and we slumped down on the floor to tea.

Even without the maps and globe that the library once held, in the isolation of those weeks I began to figure out where and who I was. I knew none of the neighbors, and the cold winter weather kept our contacts down to a minimum. I knew what it was to live in a house alone, but this time the extreme emptiness of the situation, in contrast to the clutter of the Dutton place and Ida's house, opened me up at that moment and in the years to come to big and small dramas of the country. Here, I've watched turkey vultures circle over the road, their wing spans cutting the air, landing, their talons clutching a squirrel, stiff in the ditch. I rounded up a whole herd of stray Holsteins on Christmas Eve, securing them in my pasture, the gate shut tight, only to rise the next morning to find them vanished, gone without a trace like Santa's reindeer.

I watched a khaki duck build a nest and lay six eggs under the lilac bush, then for over a week attempt to fight off the chickens, who pecked and finally destroyed five would-be ducklings. I watched the khaki sit on her remaining egg another day, then in a weird reversal and surrender to forces of nature, turn on her own young and peck that last egg to oblivion herself. I watched a rooster sit on a nest. I watched tadpoles hatch from eggs. I watched a turkey ride on Emily's back, then dismount and chase Magic into the pond and away from his hens. I watched the chrysalis of a monarch attach itself to the dorsal side of a milkweed leaf, then push out of its confinement, one glistening black leg, then another. I watched the legs of horses lifting proudly into the air or pulling buggies down the road, the weather turning hot again, a whole family jammed into the carriage, seven or eight people at once, a little boy's bare foot sticking out, the strains of harmonica music washing back over my schoolhouse.

Miriam taught me to predict rain from the wash of red light on the horizon of sunset, and I learned how that horizon was formed, from which glacial plain. I learned the soil type and the names of the prairie grasses, quickly becoming adept at spotting little and big bluestem grasses in the ditches, remnants of the prairie that had covered this region for hundreds of thousands of cycling seasons, remnants of a prairie that was almost completely destroyed in just sixty years. I read about how a Native American woman who had lost her knitting needles improvised from a set of big blue stem grasses, how the Chippewa used the grass as medicine for indigestion and stomach pains, how the Omaha made a concoction of the lower leaf blades to treat general debility from an unknown cause. I sensed what these vast fields had been like before they were planted and cultivated, how the roots of the prairie grasses sank down into the soil eight to ten feet deep, and how they made the perfect harbingers for another grass—King Corn.

I perfected my own corn crops, my own cultivations, my garden changing and developing each year. Instead of moving "forward" as most gardeners do, searching through catalogues for more and more specialized hybrid seeds, I moved "backward," thumbing through the Seed Savers yearbook, cracking the code to make contact with gardeners just a few counties away, receiving heirloom, nonhybrid seed from them in little smudged, recycled envelopes. Their successful crop, their seed became mine, and mine went back into the envelopes again. What once grew and did well in conditions very similar to mine reproduced itself. The science of the narrow niche became supreme. In order to understand the larger world, to satisfy that adolescent longing to commune with the bigger scene, I learned that I had to understand the smaller realm, the anatomy and physiology of "my own backyard."

"Home is where you know what's going on," Greg Brown, a friend, fellow Iowan, and folk singer said to me once when he moved from Minneapolis back to Iowa. "And I'm heading home."

Inside my current home, the curtains went up on the day-to-day life of Fairview School. From Max, Mahlon, and Duane, I heard about the regimens of reading, writing, and arithmetic. The switch from speaking Deutsch to English, the figuring of sums. From Fannie, Lydia, and Esther, I heard about pounding chalkboard erasers, and hauling in water, keeping the woodbox filled. The exploits of their youth flooded their faces with memories, returning them to the glow of their childhood. Their childhood became mine and mine theirs. Fairview School—with its pages of mental scrapbooks opening and closing like wings, gliding in the wind—became a place to land. Joshua became Rudy, Duane became Ott, Mac became Bud,

Bill became Bill. Esther became Ida, who became Olga. At once, Moses and Miriam became my parents and grandparents. Donna and Stu became the aunt and uncle I never had. Frogs became princes. The wind became water became earth became flame.

"Having any trouble with that well?" Max asked.

"Yes, it's been filling up with water."

"I was one of the eighth-grade boys assigned to climb down into the pit to bail it out."

"Want me to paint that flagpole, too?" Duane asked.

"That would be great."

"I used to have to shimmy up that thing with the flag at dawn. Whew, that metal could be cold on a winter morning."

"I spent most of my time down here," Mahlon said on the cellar steps.

"Here?"

"Yup, this is where the bad boys had to go and sit."

Up and down those men and women went. And up and down the road the buggies drove, pulling into my lane, my neighbors knocking to ask if they could stick their heads in the door and see "what you done with the schoolhouse." One fall night, I sat around the dining-room table at Moses and Miriam's, their whole family home for an auction, and listened to their reminiscences about their schoolhouse. Most of all, they recalled holidays. They remembered descending those cellar steps, the lights out on Halloween night, their hearts thumping, the older boys hiding under the landing, grabbing the younger children's legs as they entered the basement "spook house." They remembered boiling a gooey mixture in a huge kettle, then pulling it out, watching it harden into round, sugary candies for Christmas. They remembered shoving the desks to the side and building a tiny platform for the pageant, their parts memorized and running through their heads.

"I walked out on the stage," one of Moses and Miriam's daughters said, "pulled back the tiny curtain we strung across the room, and said my line: 'We'll have pork chops and sauerkraut on Christmas Day.' I'll never forget that. Somehow they couldn't get a turkey, so they had pork chops and sauerkraut on Christmas Day. All the parents were there at night, little presents left for the teacher on her desk, the lights shining brightly through the windows. Every time I go by at night now and see the lights lit up, I know it's you in there, but it always reminds me of Christmas."

In a sense, every night has been Christmas in Fairview School, with many gifts bestowed upon me. What have I been given? A home. A place to experience the dramas of my own internal growth. A place to find a sense of place, to feel grounded both physically and spiritually. A place to feel confidence in myself develop with my confidence to nurture plants and animals. A place to nurture myself and build up my bodily and psychological defenses. A place, as a single woman, to find a community, a group of people that made me feel part of a family again. A place where even as an outsider with strange ways and a strange illness, I found acceptance. A place to find strength in solitude, connection in being alone. Here, I've discovered that only alone could I heal, could I feel both intense physical and psychic pain and then relief. Here, as I've entered middle age, I've felt all the grief, all the exuberance of my youth descend in a single evening, only to float out again the next morning, the cool fall breezes reminding me that we all migrate up and down, and down and up again.

Last Christmas, my friend the English lord gave me a large red and green candle. Every night I light it and stare into its flames, letting the glow carry me into a trance, the wax never seeming to melt, the candle never burning out. Instead, I watch the yellow flame turn to a deep orange; then wings open and all the past spirits of this house enter again, all the little boys and girls with their books in straps, all their sleds leaning against the side of the building, all the teachers with apples on their desks, all the parents here once a year for the pageant, standing in the back of the room, their necks straining to get a glimpse of their children. I feel a convergence of people, a synchronization of lessons learned, of daily exercises and chores, of hopes and aspirations soaring in and out of this room, heavenward, toward the one bright star.

Places and Displacement: Rattlesnakes in Cyberspace

Kathleen Norris

Place can stick to us in western South Dakota. Walking past the high school on a wet fall day, it is easy to tell which of the cars belong to the country kids. They're caked with mud up to the windows, having come the twenty miles or so to town on slick gumbo and gravel roads.

It's easy to lose track of place, too. My friend Alvie in the nursing home talks often of her ranch house on the Grand River. She says, laughing almost but more in wonder, "I can't remember if we sold it, or if it's standing there empty. But I sure like to picture it, and the wild plums in spring. I remember it all the time." Periodically, she'll ask me, "Is this Lemmon or Morristown," the town some twenty-five miles to the east, which is where she lived as a child, where she moved when she and her husband retired. Alvie has misplaced her place, but in the far reaches of her mind, it still comforts her.

Alvie tells me that her father always told her she was my grandfather Totten's first patient when he got off the train in Morristown in 1909. Of course the town knew a doctor was coming, and her father had been lying in wait. He grabbed him and took him straight to the apartment above their

Copyright 1995 by Kathleen Norris

hardware store, where Alvie lay ill with both measles and pneumonia. He stayed with the family three days, which of course they never forgot. Stories like this place me here, as do the graves of the two small boys in our family plot in the Lemmon cemetery. My grandfather had been unable to save his own sons in the influenza epidemics of the teens and early twenties. Somewhere in the dusty shelves of the house are their photographs, toddlers playing in the yard, being dandled on my grandmother Totten's knee.

To be an American is to move on, to outrun change. To attach oneself to place is to surrender to it. The space I was born into in Washington, D.C., is now a parking garage; the hospital, like most urban medical centers, has for years been following its Manifest Destiny, building bigger and better buildings surrounded by miles of parking.

Miraculously, the field across from our ranch-style house in Beach Park, Illinois, between Waukegan and Zion, where we lived until I was eleven, is still being farmed. Chicago's development seems to have gone more to the south and west. That field gave me my first, uneasy taste of earth. Bigger kids, or at least the ones with more daring, used to sneak in under the barbed-wire fence, and one day in spring I decided to go there myself. I must have been seven or eight years old. I had no idea how steep the furrows would be, how far down my feet would sink into the rich, moist earth. All I could think of was the folktale about the girl who trod on a loaf, being too vain to soil her new shoes. I wasn't wearing new shoes—I wasn't that foolish—but I was certain that I'd done enough proud and cruel things to be punished just as that girl was, and be taken deep underground. With great fear and trembling I got out of that field by myself, and never went back.

Hawaii is the next place I remember well, as my family moved there in 1959, just before statehood, and has remained ever since. I graduated from high school in Honolulu. It doesn't take long, in Hawaii, to register the dramatic, usually dreadful impact of change. I remember when the Honolulu airport was one room, a hangar open on both ends. You went in the front door to buy your ticket and a flower lei, and walked out the back onto the tarmac to board your plane. I remember when the site of the vast Ala Moana shopping center was a lovely swamp, full of birds whose names I never knew. When Robert Louis Stevenson lived in a hut in Waikiki, he used to walk through this swamp on his way to and from downtown Honolulu.

When I was a college student, I once had a job in the library of the Bishop Museum. There, under the vigilant eye of Miss Margaret C. Titcomb, I labeled glass negatives of Honolulu that had been taken around the turn of the century. I knew the city well by then and was shocked to discover that many busy, downtown intersections had once been streambeds with flower-laden banks. The streams had been paved, or made to run underground. I gained a new respect for the power of money, of business interests, to simply sweep place away.

Like many young writers from other places, I lived for a time in New York City. The hothouse atmosphere of its literary world was not necessarily good for my writing at the time, but there have been residual benefits. Most important is the respect I gained for poetry as an oral art form, listening to readings by poets as diverse as W. H. Auden, Richard Howard, Denise Levertov, Robert Lowell, Adrienne Rich, Tömas Transtromer, Diane Wakoski, Richard Wilbur, and James Wright.

I won a first-book competition during those years; a book full of strange music and promise as well as some awful, sophomoric verse. I was sophisticated the way only a person in her twenties can be, and both I and my poetry suffered for it. It wasn't until I had moved to the place of my childhood summers, my grandparents' house, where my mother grew up, that my voice as a writer emerged. And over eight years, I wrote another book of poems. A writer who knew that book but had recently stumbled across my first book in a used book store, said to me, "When you moved to South Dakota, it's like you discovered gravity."

This is a journey many writers have made. Feeling a call to go back to the matrix of the family stories, we place ourselves in their landscape. For me that is the western Dakotas. It has shaped my work for more than twenty years. I am placed here, maybe not the way my friend Tom Lyman is, who in his late seventies still lives on the ranch he was born on, but deep enough. Yet, even though I have not followed the college teaching route of many writers—I live 100 miles from the nearest small college, more than

400 from a university of any size—I am also a person of the literary culture, and it places me here in a distinct way. If you will, it displaces me.

The fact that so much of my work is directed outward, to publications, colleges, and organizations in the urban Midwest and East, can't help but set me apart from the people I live with in an agriculturally based society. And my perceptions of them, and the place in which I live, can't help but be altered by links with the world outside that are a necessary part of surviving as a writer in isolated circumstances—modem, fax, FedEx, and my preferred "snail mail." Often I am a stunned observer of the ways in which my worlds collide. The first time I had a poem printed in the *New Yorker*, I was startled to hear the Presbyterian pastor in Lemmon announce it in church on Sunday, as one of the "joys of the congregation." His gesture made me more a part of the Lemmon community, even as it separated me from it.

Having to frequently come and go from Lemmon, as most of my paying work is elsewhere, has reinforced my sense both of rootedness and displacement. It's because I'm acclimated to the relative calm of my small town that I usually enjoy (at least for a few days) the sound of traffic in the charged-up, urban intensity of midtown Minneapolis or Manhattan. I enjoy the feel of being an anonymous one among many on a crowded sidewalk or subway platform. And sometimes I am enlarged by unexpected connections that surface, linking the urban and the rural. During the Gulf War in 1991, I happened to be in New York City, and my conversations with cab drivers centered on the young people we knew who'd been sent to fight. Urban poor, rural poor, for whom the military represents opportunity.

One day this summer I was part of a conference call among poets scattered across America. To begin, our chair had asked us to "go around the room," a cyberspace room, stretching from California and Oregon all the way to Connecticut and Upstate New York. I stretched out in a favorite rocker to take the call. Just a few days before, near the crest of a butte some forty miles from Lemmon, a place with a view of nearly sixty miles to the south and west, my body had been totally absorbed in giving a rattlesnake enough room. I'd scared him up at dusk, after a spectacular sunset, and while I couldn't see the snake at all, instinct told me where his rattling had come from and I quickly backed off.

It was a good night, all in all, and even the rattlesnake's presence felt like a blessing, a West River welcome after I'd spent nearly a year in Minnesota, writing up a storm and consorting with trees and lakes, blue herons and loons. All is forgiven, the rattlesnake said; watch your step.

I received another kind of welcome at a social and hymn-sing held at Hope Church, a country church I love. It sits in the middle of a pasture, and as the pickup trucks were arriving I was hugging everyone in sight—people I hadn't seen for many months, ranch men and women in their best jeans and snakeskin cowboy boots, some moving stiffly, seemingly suddenly older, little kids who seemed to have grown about a mile, new babies. We were also keeping an eye on the sky. It was overcast, so it didn't seem as if the sunset would amount to much. Wait a few minutes, one of the old-timers said. Soon the eastern sky turned pink, bathing our faces in rosy light. I had my back to the west when I *felt* the light change, as if I'd been nudged on the shoulder by an unseen hand. It was as if the light had spoken. I turned to a horizon ablaze with deep scarlet; the upper sky had turned to fine-spun gold. When the night settled in and mosquitoes came out we went inside the church and sang with gusto the hymns of our childhoods: "Amazing Grace," "I Would Be True," "I Love to Tell the Story." Welcome home.

One hot, windy day in early fall, my husband and I had to leave Lemmon for a trip to Denver. The nearest airport, in Bismarck, North Dakota, is 130 miles away and we'd arranged to ride with a friend in his pickup truck. Since Jim, born and bred in the country, had said he felt like taking "the whiskey roads" into town, we tied our suitcases in plastic garbage bags before tossing them into the back of the truck. A hundred miles of gravel road can kick up a lot of dust.

We took off from Lemmon on the "black and blue," appropriately named for the quality of the ride it gives a body, and drove through hamlets like Bentley and Almont, accessible only on the country roads. Jim could keep to a steady seventy-five miles an hour without ever seeing a patrolman (our only traffic was a handful of farm vehicles). With the cab windows wide open and the temperature rising—it neared ninety degrees that afternoon—we each drank a pint of cold water en route and still felt dehydrated when we arrived in Bismarck. Our faces were creased with dust.

But we didn't think of the trip in terms of hardship; it was simply how we were traveling that day, how Jim travels most days in his construction work. The reward in all of this was experiencing all over again the incredible roominess of western Dakota, seeing signs a person would miss from the highway. Along one fifteen-mile stretch we passed the remains of stone houses and barns, all highly skilled rubble construction, no mortar. This told us that the area had been settled by people from a particular region— probably a particular village, in the Old Country—Scandinavia, or the steppes of Russia. The people who built those walls are probably dead; by now their children may have retired to prefab houses in a nearby town. "Someone went to a shitload of work," Jim said, his voice bitter. "And then they just let it all go." It is sad to see all that skilled human work, hard work, left to the elements, but that's Dakota. One might say, that's life.

Another, less mixed pleasure of the trip was the chance to visit with Jim, a friend from our early days out here. We seldom see him anymore because he's moved to Bismarck to make a living. He was curious about how my life had been going since *Dakota* was published early in 1993. It's full of craziness, I told him. I had my mail in a canvas bag on my lap and partly for his amusement I sorted through it. Invitations from colleges, clergy groups, and book clubs inviting me to come to Oregon, Montana, Nebraska, Indiana, South Carolina to give a talk or a reading were an ironic reminder of the curious situation I am in right now. Having written about a place because I love it, I could now spend all my time on the road talking about it, losing not only my sanity but any sense of where it is I belong.

There was also a solicitation from a poetry magazine, a rejection note from another, several letters responding to *Dakota*, galleys from a publisher hoping for a blurb, and one fax that I'd picked up on the way out of town, an edited copy of a book review I'd written for the *New York Times*. "All these people managed to ignore me for twenty years when I just wrote poetry," I said. "I'm paying for the sin of writing prose." Jim was philosophical. He gave the *Times* logo a quick glance. "Look on the bright side, Kathleen," he said. "When Dan Quayle comes looking for the Cultural Elite, he'll never find you here." Just then we saw a golden eagle overhead.

Homing In

Jack Driscoll

I still feel a dull ache in my stomach, an emptiness when I remember the lines in *Myths & Texts* where Gary Snyder says that the kids grow up and go to college and don't come back. Not for long they don't, not usually.

"But *you* will," my mother insisted. "You will." She sold real estate, and our family would help maintain the national average by moving every two or three years, but never very far. One time into the green-shuttered house next door on Orchard Street, then two blocks over to Keef Avenue. These were the mid-1950s, and "subdivision" would have sounded like some dark, unknowable math. Holyoke was still a town of neighborhoods. We never changed schools or lost our friends.

"You'll come back home," she said again, and when I waved good-bye I had this blurry-eyed vision of Thomas Wolfe standing on our front porch and shaking his head no behind her. He looked like an angel and like a ghost, white like the timber wolf who was carried a hundred miles downriver in a flood and somehow found his way back to the fold. It's a story I was told as a kid, and I suddenly remembered that beautiful William Stafford poem about the salmon who slip into the sea and are gone for

Copyright 1995 by Jack Driscoll

years, but always return. I thought about Herakles and Jason and mostly about Odysseus, the greatest of all travelers home, and about the deep and sad and, as I've known it, the very adult malady of homesickness.

Even my ex-wife, who wanted some honest distance between us, said, "Don't go out to the Midwest, don't go there." She said it was barren and flat and full of Bibles. She insisted the people were fifteen years behind us, and I flashed on them on a Saturday night, dancing in the basements of churches—the hully gully and the Bristol stomp.

But I'd already signed the contract to teach at a coed boarding school in Michigan, a place I'd never been and didn't much want to be. Hadn't I already made my stand here in western Massachusetts at the edge of the Berkshires, buying and renovating a century-and-a-half-old farmhouse? Slate roof and fieldstone foundation. Hand-hewn chestnut timbers, a Dutch-oven fireplace. And two barns, one with a stained glass window above the hayloft and a view of the Connecticut River Valley so spectacular in all seasons that I'm certain Frederick Church would have painted it had he ever looked down from that mountain. I've saved a photograph or two, but I don't haul them out much anymore.

And I don't think often about the retired air force colonel who rented the farm on a one-year lease. He was tall and polite and said he wouldn't pester me a thousand miles away for nitpicky repairs and he never did, not once. He said he had a wife and two kids but no pets, then his Saint Bernard scratched holes large enough through the front and back doors to let herself in and out. I have no idea how long this scratching took. The colonel defaulted on three months' rent before he disappeared for good and I drove back home after that one year away to a summer of repairs and then put the farm up for sale, and I wouldn't return again, not for a single visit, for almost a decade.

But that's getting out ahead of the story. For now, it's still 1975, and yes, I've decided the smart career move is to "get one academic foot in the door," even if it's only a high school, and it is, after all, my one and only job offer, though for three consecutive years I've scattered hundreds of copies of my skimpy résumé around the country: Chattanooga; Anchorage; Monroe, Louisiana. A poet/professor/mentor of mine quoted Roethke when I asked for advice about holding fast or moving on: "I dream of journeys repeatedly," he said, and reminded me that Roethke was a Michigan boy, a romantic connection for a romantic like me. And anyway, he was curious to know, what was a year or two to a guy still in his twenties with only one slim chapbook and a handful of "little magazine" publications? All apprentice poems, I'd realize later, grad-school poems with the life workshopped right out of them.

And I'd been writing nothing since being hired by an older, quiet man named Warren LaPalme who mostly sat in his truck and listened to the Red Sox on the radio while I slid on my back into crawl space after crawl space, stapling batts of insulation to splintery floor joists and breathing in those tiny pink particles of fiberglass. I wore a miner's light around my head, and sometimes I'd turn it off and close my eyes, arms folded across my chest, and try to imagine a life anywhere but where I was.

I arrived in heavy rain. No letup for three straight days, and I went stir crazy finally in the knotty-pine-walled cabin I'd rented from the school, classes still two weeks away. A ghost community. So I drank rum and cranked up Bob Dylan's "Sad-Eyed Lady of the Lowlands," a guaranteed crying-jag combo, my Chevrolet pickup still half unpacked and backed up close to the door, a full tank of gas.

But I believe in omens and signs, and when the sky cleared before the bottle emptied, I took a walk, which, on this campus, meant into the woods—1,800 acres between two lakes, Wahbekaness and Wahbekanetta: "water lingers, water lingers again."

Nobody believes me, but I swear, lost and standing in ground fog, the harvest moon appeared from behind the clouds and illuminated a pay phone attached to the trunk of a tall white pine. Then the sweep of millions of stars, and gazing up I believed I could press the black receiver to my ear and dial God. Or at least all the earthly women I had ever loved and lost and loved again on this night after the rum and the rain.

I had no change in my pockets, no dial tone to call collect and reminisce long distance, and for as long as it took to steady my heart's clumsy stammering, I listened instead to the voice of the wind through the trees—I actually sat cross-legged like a drunken monk on the wet needles and considered my life until just before dawn.

I did not read Basho or Han Shan after a long, hot shower, followed by a cold one to clear my head—so it was neither of those ancients who inspired the line that would become my first poem in almost two years, and a keeper: "the way a tree dreams light into its skin." I drew the shades against the sun and fell into deep sleep.

I've been trying to flesh out a short story: a man my age, almost fifty, keeps shoveling snow from the roof of his trailer house, while inside, under the dull, yellowish haze of a bare light bulb above the kitchen table, his only son—let's say he's fourteen—studies a color brochure for a summer space camp in Texas. Or maybe, in a slightly altered version, the man has just finished, so he leans on his shovel and stares up at the moon and the stars and then he shakes off one of his gloves and lights a cigarette and thinks again about his wife who has recently left him. At this moment in the moonlight I imagine that the trim on the trailer house is pink, and that the man is a decent man but a bad drinker, though I have not discovered yet how long he's gone without a drink—half an hour? All day? How about six months? Perhaps custody of his son depends on the man's sobriety, though who would drive out so late on a night like this to check?

I like what Freud says about there being no jokes. Take this one, for example: We have only three seasons in northern Michigan—July, August, and winter. And so a man has been shoveling snow from his roof, a ladder leaning against his trailer house, the temperature at minus thirty. In Wolf Lake, a few miles away, there's a bar with a sign that says just that— BAR—in red neon, and two snowmobiles parked behind the largest wind-blown and shell-sculpted drift. And a woman bending over the broken Wurlitzer as if even the faded song titles were music enough.

"Such unpoetic lives," a woman once said to me after a reading I'd given at a college back East. Not the kind of folks, I agreed, who'd travel, as I did, hundreds of miles downstate in search of Theodore Roethke's house. The fisherman/hunter friend of mine I asked for directions said only that Saginaw was closer to Ohio than to Michigan.

This is the north country. The bridge across the Mackinac Straits is the longest suspension bridge in the world, connecting the landmass of lower Michigan to the Upper Peninsula (referred to as the U. P.). It was there I watched a black bear gorge himself into blissful intoxication on service berries—I could smell the fermentation downwind of him where I sat for over an hour until he wandered off. And I'm thinking about William Stafford again, who said that it takes many miles to equal one wildcat. But I've seen wildcats in the U. P., and I want desperately to believe that wolves are making a comeback, too, that the choruses of coyotes at night are prayer-songs we hear in our animal hearts.

There are towns named Painsdale and Christmas and Mass City and De Tour Village. A U. P. petition to secede from the rest of the state is still alive with signatures to preserve this wilderness. I met a woman who said if she could sign every day she would, and every day it would be with another name: waxwing, mountain ash, inner-dune, mink frog, sweet fern. Sedge wren, she said, and fox grape and badger. It had turned very cold, and she said winter solstice. She said snow owl.

Trespasser, visitor, sojourner, resident, native—my burrowing in has gone something like this, though maybe native *spirit* will be all I can honestly claim in the end. If so, it will no doubt be enough.

Over dinner one evening I talked with an architect whose name I had been given by a mutual friend. I needed someone with enough imagination to design a house to fit this oddly shaped piece of high ground. He told me he couldn't do the job because he had recently suffered a heart attack, but then all of a sudden he became inexpensively available because (this is true) I could recite from memory lengthy passages from Thoreau. And did as we walked the land the next morning. And about the house, he said, we'll build up.

My study overlooks the Little Betsie River, which is not so little. Slow-moving and six feet deep in the deepest holes, it winds through thousands of acres of wetlands, breeding ground for wood ducks and mallards. I can canoe from the house to school, or upriver away from it, as my wife, a native Midwesterner, and I did earlier this summer. Neither of us could sleep, and so we paddled, she still in her nightgown, up into Bridge Lake after midnight to watch the brilliant showers of the northern lights. We uncorked and drank a ritzy bottle of Bordeaux we'd been saving for an occasion I don't recall anymore. But this much is clear: we leaned toward each other half a dozen times, clinking glasses as we toasted our lives.

It's already October, and for the past half hour the blue heron has kept his outpost at the first bend, knee-deep in shallows. But now he spreads his enormous wings and rises slow-motion, gliding downriver above the last of the cardinal flowers: blue heron, red cardinal flowers. I'm reminded of the peace of wild things that Wendell Berry writes about. Some mornings, while staring out on all of this, I actually believe that I might say something eternal.

But don't misunderstand—since Blake, I have lost all patience with the voices of mystics. My excuse today is that we're nearing the end of another millennium, so I'll risk that tone—I'll say that this is the only place where I've ever felt true faith as a writer, the love and connection to a spirit beyond myself. The world expands to consume the ego, and everything comes more and more alive.

Close attentiveness over time, and now that twenty years have elapsed, I have been trying to interpret something universal about that man on the roof and the sadness he feels. It's my sadness, of course—I know that the heron will migrate south on the next bad weather, predicted to arrive this week. Because herons mate for life, he will return alone again next spring after ice-out. And joke or no joke, we've got all that winter to wait for him, all that snow to shovel.

But the roof is clear to the tar paper, and there's a path out to the car, which may or may not start—I haven't decided yet, and it can't be important yet anyway, not until the county plow comes through and there's somewhere to go, or a route the man's wife can follow home if she's changed her mind, though there's almost no chance of that. At best she might call, so maybe that's why the boy is still not in bed, his father watching him and shivering just outside the thin perimeter light of the window. He believes just one stiff hit of whiskey would warm him up, and I think he's right, it would. There's half a pint of Old Museum stashed between the mattress and box spring, and a late night fight on the black-and-white Sylvania in his narrow bedroom—middleweights, about his size. Or here's a better idea: no matter how the man tinkers with the rabbit ears and vertical hold, he keeps losing the reception until the screen completely fills with static. Like snow, he thinks, and closes the door and sits at the foot of the bed and drinks between rounds. The audio is distant and scratchy—the only clear sound is the bell, and each time it rings he begins to bob and weave, believing, until the moment the fight is stopped, that he has slipped every single punch, and finally countered with one big overhand right for the knockout. But when he hears his son leave the kitchen without saying good night, there is no victory. Just a man almost fifty who stumbles into the bathroom and turns on the light and leans into the mirror. You can see, from his puffy, bloodshot eyes, and by the way he steadies himself with both hands on the rim of the sink, that he has no real illusions about who he is, about who has taken the pounding.

Roland Merullo, in his novel *Leaving Losapas*, says, "You loved or hated a place because you loved or hated yourself in that place." True, of course. But I have also hated myself in this place I love, hated myself for waiting so long to travel back home.

1983. A good year because my first full-length collection of poems has just been published. Some early, good reviews, a few book signings scheduled in the Midwest next spring. Magazine editors soliciting poems from me for the first time. It feels like the real thing, though I did not say "poet" when the guy sitting next to me in business class asked, "What do you do?" For the sake of keeping a conversation alive, I said, "teacher," which immediately made him feel superior and relaxed, talkative. He even bought me a beer.

But I've brought copies of my book, presents for the family, and my oldest sister has already met me at the airport in Hartford, and we've driven the twenty miles back to her house in suburban Longmeadow where I wait for my mother to arrive for the Christmas meal. It's a feast, really: cherrystones and blue tips and jumbo shrimp. New England clam chowder. My younger sister is here from Mystic, Connecticut—until an hour ago, I had never seen her daughter Brie, who is six years old and asleep in my arms. My identical twin brother's son looks more than a little like me when I was his age: freckles on his nose and cheeks, a cowlick where my hair has since receded away. I have a lot of gray for someone my age, a trait from my mother's side—early Rheaume gray—and my heartbeat speeds up when I hear her knocking on the front door. For the few long seconds it takes her to enter, I believe it's my grandmother back from the dead—the resemblance is so startling that I close my eyes, and when I open them she is standing in the center of the living room, staring at me. She has not even taken off her coat, and the family has gone so suddenly silent around us that I can hear the bubblers on the Christmas tree beside me. My younger sister, who does not cry easily, cries now as she lifts her sleeping child, and I rise into what is the clearest and saddest and most beautiful moment of my life. A kind of stop-time, everything animate and inanimate frozen around us until we both step forward, and then the telephone rings and someone starts the stereo—Bing Crosby singing "Joy to the World," and my mother, hugging and hugging me, whispers, "I always knew it, I always knew you'd come home."

I agree to spend the night in my old bedroom, but I can't sleep. Every time I begin to drift off I see the ghost of Thomas Wolfe again, still shaking his head. So I get up and drift like a sleepwalker down the stairs. He's sitting in a chair, the lamp on, and he says, "Go ahead," but I know there's not a single item I can touch that will not shatter in my hands. I notice he's balancing the glass figurine of a unicorn in his palm, holding it out to me, and all I can do is turn away. But wherever I look, the feeling is the same—that's me at sixteen, smiling from behind the glass of the stand-up frame. I'm holding a pickerel on a stringer, holding it forward to the lens so the fish seems bigger than it was in this moment of victory. And now everything begins to enlarge the longer I stare—it's dizzying, and I have to sit down on the couch across the room from Thomas Wolfe, and raise my hands in surrender. I am a stranger in this house.

And strangely relaxed by that admission. And exhausted from the criss-crossing of emotions all day. My mother walks halfway down the stairs and asks if I am okay.

"Yes," I say, and it's the affirmation of that single sound—*yes*—that confirms, not only this moment eternal, but the passing of this moment into the next and the next, which I do not remember. They have dissolved into the light and permanence of this other.

Have I mentioned how tightly her hands gripped the railing? How the white rungs spiraled past her into the dark?

I've been sitting for hours, observing the world outside my window. And daydreaming again, which has become more and more my process of writing. Silence and time.

I'm thinking back across some distance, a reviewer referring to me as a "Michigan snow poet." I wasn't quite sure how to take that, but I know now that he identified early on how consuming this region would become as the physical backdrop for my work over the next two decades. And perhaps it also identified the lack of intense interior landscape, memory's place in all of this—one landscape balancing and informing the other:

Building the Cold from Memory

Winter without its story.
After all, no one has arrived
unless the first snow is ready to speak,
unless the book dropped in the field
is discovered beneath the horse's feet.

What we have dreamed is only ash in the stove.
And whispering to ourselves about the cold
will not matter for many years,
not until our children shiver,
undressing themselves in strange bedrooms.

For now the wind will sort out its missing gloves
and hold the barn door hinges silent a little while.
If we listen

our fathers might drag a block of ice for the last time
on a sled.

> That's enough to begin.
> Even without the stars
> someone keeps ringing a heavy bell,
> the distant voice of a buoy praying on the far shore.

I was beginning finally to discover what Wordsworth meant by "something more deeply interfused." Snow, after all, is snow only until there's a human presence—indeed it is not even snow until there is someone to confront it and give it a name: snow, silence, solitude, loneliness, madness, desire. Like the man left staring into his bathroom mirror. Or like his son, who feels so disconnected from everything here that he dreams only of launching pads and spaceships and blasting off for other galaxies.

But I'm staying put for the long haul in this house on the river. Because the hawthorn berries are finally ripe, four partridge keep bending the limbs of the bush almost to the ground as they feed. It has turned cold and windy, orange and red maple leaves floating by like tiny boats. I have to get up and go close all the windows, and when I do I walk downstairs and outside to the road to check the mailbox. I'm awaiting word on a story I've sent to a magazine, but the only envelope today contains my frequent flier mileage summary. I'm close to another free ticket, which I'll use to fly back to Massachusetts for Thanksgiving. The miles, I think, accumulate like snow, like years, or even lifetimes. So let another winter come. Let it take us where it will.

Recovering the Past

Stewards of Memory

Martha Bergland

My brothers and sister and I grew up on a farm in Illinois, on land so flat that only little children who rode bicycles on it and farmers who drove tractors over the wet spots knew that there were subtle rises and falls. It was not a land easy to romanticize, though sometimes the weather did that for us. I don't remember that we ever talked about "the land" or "the prairie," but there was a lot of talk about and admiration for the extremes of weather—the black fronts that we watched come out of the west like destiny, strange mild mists that fuzzed all the trees with frost, thunderstorms we got up in the night to watch, drifting in our pajamas like ghosts from window to window in the dark house. And the sunset turned the usual harsh light to something romantic in its gilding of each fence post and cornstalk, romantic in its purples and reds and greens, which, if translated into emotions, would have been difficult to speak of among farmers and farmers' wives. But in most light on most days, everything was revealed; nothing seemed hidden or mysterious. There were no extremes of emotion or expression—no fear or wonder or awe.

In my family we thought the romantic was necessary. So all seven of us,

Copyright 1995 by Martha Bergland

I believe, daydreamed of woods and lakes and valleys and curving rivers. My mother had grown up in the pine woods of Louisiana and my father in Delaware near the Brandywine River, so when we went for drives along Salt Creek and the Sangamon River, they were probably thinking of the woods they remembered, but we children had never had woods. We felt deprived on that flat square-mile farm, without even an old orchard, a falling-down barn, a winding creek to play near. We did pretty well with the drainage ditch a half a mile from the house, but even the word tells you: a ditch is not the same as a creek.

Still, that square place was our home and now that I live in Wisconsin, in a wooded, hilly place near Lake Michigan and the Milwaukee River, I miss the flat land. I know it's perverse and common to appreciate what you had only when you don't have it anymore, but here you can't see far enough. You can't just look out the west window and see what the weather will be tomorrow; you have to watch television news for that. None of us lives on the farm now; the farm is sold and I think all of us miss it at least a little. We live in California and Oregon and Vermont and Wisconsin, so maybe our dreams for more romantic places have all come true.

Like many, and now perhaps most, middle-class American families, no two consecutive generations of my family for six generations have lived in the same house or on the same farm, in the same town or even the same part of the country. Yet each generation must wish for its children what Yeats prayed for his daughter, that she might she live like a green laurel, "rooted in one dear perpetual place." But it seems the only "dear perpetual place" we are rooted in is in memory—and odd patches of that.

The earliest Swedish relative whose name my family knows is Olf Knall, who was born at Hasenbruk in Hälsingland in Sweden in 1795. Olf Knall was the second husband of his wife, whose name we don't know, and it was her land that Olf farmed; it was her home in which their son Anders Berglund was born in 1814.

At eighteen, when Anders joined the Swedish army to fulfill his military service, he had to choose, as was customary, a "soldier name." Anders named himself *Berglund*—"mountain grove"—after the place where he was born, the place his mother and father farmed. When Anders came home from the army, instead of taking again his family name, his father's name, he kept his soldier name for himself and for his many descendants. When he was an old man living in Bishop Hill, Illinois, he described his early life and his mother's farm, after which he named us:

> Although it is hard and rocky, it is now a beautiful place, a place where my thoughts often wander because of my childhood's happy days. It is also a romantic place. Mountains and trees—where I derive my name from. . . . The place where I was born is a natural, beautiful country on the north side of the so-called Hukna Lake from where the Hukna River flows. . . . From east to west there is a wooded mountain with the same name as the lake. Nearly a half mile up the mountain, . . . on the south side, there is a flat, round depression which has been made into a field. Outside of this flat, low place the ground is covered with pine trees. It is very stony and, on the north side, there are steep cliffs. In the center of this flat plain there is a large and deep spring which flows toward the south and falls into the lake. On the edges of this plain grow ronn, ash, and birch.

I have never seen this place Anders Berglund described, but I believe he has given us enough detail so that, even today, we could find it. And we can imagine it: The sun warms those south-facing slopes. The pine woods scent the path he must have taken as a boy to work that low, damp bowl of a field. In the fall of the year the yellow of the birch and ash lights the field, and in spring the delicate new leaves hang like moths against the dark of the evergreens. How welcome and strange is the bone-chilling cold of that spring that wells up in the middle of the rocky field and flows down to the Hukna Lake. The land itself must have been easy on the eye, but hard on the shoulders and the back. Anders says, "The little farm was not large enough to supply food for us all, especially as the crops often failed and as my father often had to be away in the summer and work as a soldier for his country."

"It was a romantic place." The discomfort of it and the disappointment in it were surpassed in his memory by its beauty, by its association with the romantic.

What does he mean when he calls a place romantic? Though in the fifties in Illinois we didn't and wouldn't use the word *romantic*, that is what we longed for—a romantic place. And I think I know what that was.

In a romantic place there was mystery; all was not visible at once. The road disappeared, not on the horizon, but beyond a bend, beyond a stand of trees. A romantic place would have complexity beyond sky, bean field, ditch. There is, of course, all the complexity one could wish for in the whorled and speckled and spiked detail of the prairie and the subtle changes of light and color, but those subtleties were lost on us kids who drew pictures with rickrack mountains, oval lakes, branching broccoli trees. You can't draw a prairie and we didn't have words for what we saw beyond field, sky, cloud, road, and all the colors named in the Crayola box. We thought we lacked the complexity of a mysterious landscape, but it was really language we lacked.

We wanted to be in places where all was not visible at once, and we wanted to see relics of the past lying around—old bridges or falling-down chicken houses or ancient willow trees. But farmers on whose places old buildings slowly crumbled and their grandfathers' fences leaned this way and that and their grandmothers' orchards splintered and rotted were thought of as lazy and inefficient, and that's putting it nicely. The ideal was a neat, trimmed place where everything was new and useful, where the grass was clipped right up to the bright white corn crib, where boundaries were clear, and nothing that wasn't productive was left standing.

We couldn't have said, Take us to a romantic place where there's old stuff lying around, but we did know to ask to be taken to a place where there was water. Usually that meant we drove to a creek down the road and parked on the one-lane bridge until another car came along. We got out and hung over the rusty iron railings and stared into the water running lazily over the mud. Minnows and water spiders and crawdads were the coin of this foreign realm and waterweeds the paper money. We felt we had to have this reflection and reversal of our upstanding world; we had to have another world to peer into, a small one to stir with a stick.

A romantic place also had to have at least a little bit of danger—a cliff you might fall off of, a pond you might drown in, a boulder that might fall on you, a woods you might never come out of. At home on the farm, Mom could send us out knowing that all danger came not from the natural, not from the place. We might get hit by Gene Olson driving that whistling car sixty-five miles an hour on our gravel road. Or we might get caught in an auger or fall off the corncrib. All the danger came from what had been made by the hand of man. There was no natural place to fall from, the ditch was usually too dry to drown in, and nothing but the pipeline plane or the big tractor wheels could fall on you. There was the crazy weather and that was dangerous and therefore romantic, but you couldn't count on the weather.

The most important quality of any romantic place for us was that it had to be apparently useless. On the farm where we lived and the farms all around us what you mainly saw were the fields, which were factories, production lines of corn and beans. So we went for drives to the low, wooded places along Friends Creek or Salt Creek or the Sangamon River, places that were too wooded or too often flooded to farm. In that part of the world, by the 1950s the only way to make a living was to raise corn or soybeans or sell things to people who did. There was no livestock, so there was no use for a pasture or a fence. There was no use for land with trees on it. Because a piece of land with trees on it was a graveyard or wasteland or a park, we spent a lot of time picnicking in cemeteries, walking on trails in parks, trespassing down by the creek.

I am sure that if my brothers and sister and I could take Anders Berglund for a drive today, we would all agree on what makes a place a romantic place.

When Anders and his wife, Brita Olson, came to America in 1847 with their three young children and with other followers of the strange Swedish preacher Erik Jansson, they left behind them Anders's mother and his mother's romantic farm. They left behind Brita Olson's five children by a previous marriage, her elderly relatives, and her valuable farm, which was much more successful than Anders's mother's rocky farm. But they were followers of Erik Jansson, described by Anders in a letter as "the faithful steward, whom the Lord appointed over all his goods, over all the blessedness there is." Anders and Brita sold her farm and gave the money to be held in common with the Jansson community. They turned the dream of the land into a dream of religious freedom and a dream of paradise.

The place they came to, Bishop Hill in western Illinois—after the first hard winter when they lived in caves dug out of the side of a hill—must have seemed like paradise. They found at this place red and white oak groves; mulberry and apple trees; grapevines; and cedar trees, which they knew only from the Bible. The land was fertile and free of rocks. There was water for power. There were deer, buffalo, geese, and ducks. There was limestone for building and clay for bricks. The Mississippi was only thirty miles west, close enough for the colonists to build a fishing camp. Olof Olsson, who had found this place after scouting in Wisconsin and Minnesota for sites for their colony, had written back to Sweden calling this "the new land of Canaan." It was a blessed land—both useful and beautiful.

At Bishop Hill the land is rolling, not so flat as where we grew up. There gentle slopes lead down to the little Edwards River, which skirts the edge of town. But the land does not roll so much that it can't be farmed; the land is good farmland—black and fertile. You could, on an early fall evening, stand on the east edge of town—200 people live there now; it's very quiet—and, if you looked south you would be looking up a gentle rise to the horizon where a long sweet curve of yellow corn met the sky. At that line where the blue sky and yellow hill meet a mile away, there is a farm with feathery big pines and the dark mass of barns and house. And between you and that farm there are two more slopes on the side of this long rise where the pheasants call out their exotic and vinegary call, and green walnuts fall into the fencerow from the adolescent trees.

If you turn to the north you are looking downhill and you see the little street blue in the evening and beyond it the dark grasses and weeds, still juicy but the seed heads are dry and rattle with grasshoppers, and the fields are pink and green in the evening light. Hidden among those trees is the brown river, about as wide as the road, where cattle and children wade. A wooded hill rises beyond it. You can see a long way, but not so far that it makes you feel "lonesome" like when you look down a power line marching away to the end of time.

At the center of the village is a wooded square park, and on one side of the square is the Colony Church, a severe white clapboard building with delicate old mullioned windows; it looks like a Shaker building. And on other sides of the square are the Steeple Building and the Colony Hotel.

Both of these are square stucco buildings three stories high built in the 1850s. They are classical and formal, but not official, somehow. The mottled stucco in tones of tan and gold and pink is too warm and too personal to allow the buildings to impose.

The Hospital Building on the western edge of the village is a Greek Revival clapboard building built in 1855. It is restored now to its original mustard yellow paint and white Doric trim. It's a wonderful building, but what you can see from it is even better. The back of the building faces west, looks out on small square fields and pastures whose fencerows are growing up to look like hedgerows. From the second-floor balcony on a humid June evening, you could watch as the mists rise and silver the still fields and gray the distant oak and maple trees that grow along the river. At your back is the village with its quiet sounds of human life and dog life and smell of supper cooking. The world from that balcony seems perfect in its scale: You could easily walk out and sit under those trees beside the quiet brown river. Though no one we know or are related to lives there now, Bishop Hill seems that it could be a realization of a dream of a "dear perpetual place"—romantic and pastoral, useful and beautiful, quiet and unchanging and gentle.

But this is not the place my brothers and sister and I dreamed of when we were children. We were brought here a few times when we were young, and we were bored. It was just another small Illinois town to children who thought they had seen enough of small Illinois towns. There was not enough drama there to make that the "scenery" we craved. Bishop Hill had no "view" where we could see four states and several mountain ranges and a blue lake. There was no cliff to worry about jumping off, no waterfall, no way to get lost in Bishop Hill, Illinois, where you could see clear through the town from any one of the intersections.

It is because of wars and economic losses and gains and marriages that we lived, not in Bishop Hill, but on a farm in east-central Illinois more than a hundred miles from this place.

When we were growing up we didn't hear much of the dramatic story of the fourteen years of the Bishop Hill Colony. I remember that our father told us a little about the prosperity of the colony, and he must have told us of the shooting of Erik Jansson by the man John Root. But we heard it as the sort of story you find on historical markers beside the highway, probably because that is the way the story was told to him. My father's grandfather, Eric Bergland, middle son of Anders and Brita, became very "American" after he went away to the Civil War, then to West Point, then married a rich woman from Kentucky. Those stories of "the old people" at "the Hill" might have faintly embarrassed him. Or else they embarrassed his wife, Lucy. Or her mother. Because only after research did I find that Anders Berglund was, for a short time after Jansson was killed, the religious leader of the colony. And only later did we find that Anders was one of the planners of that emigration of more than 2,000 people, that he was a carpenter, and later a Methodist minister. So the place of Bishop Hill was not a place we felt we were connected to, and the disconnection came with Eric. He disconnected himself from Bishop Hill and the stories associated with it, so very little of that came to us through his descendants.

What Eric Bergland did leave us was our name. He changed the spelling of his name from Berglund to Bergland during the Civil War; Bergland was *his* soldier name. And he left us his Civil War diaries. But it was his wife, Lucy Scott McFarland, from Lexington, Kentucky, who left her son, my grandfather, the square-mile section that later my father farmed, where my brothers and sister and I grew up.

Eric Bergland was born in 1844 in Sweden. He was three years old when his parents brought him to Illinois. He was six when Eric Jansson was shot and killed, and his father became, for a short time, spiritual leader of the colony. He was six and seven when talk of the California Gold Rush swept the colony, when many of the leaders set out for the West—to escape the vengeance of Root and to strike it rich for the indebted colony. As a young boy Eric was set to work in the colony print shop in nearby Galva, Illinois. He was managing that small print shop when he and many other Swedes from the area enlisted for service in the Civil War. He was seventeen when he went away to war—even younger than his father and grandfather had been. But unlike them, he loved the army and made it his career.

After the War of 1812, before Eric Bergland was born, the McFarlands were buying land in Illinois from veterans who had been given 160 acres by the government to encourage them to settle that territory. The McFarlands acquired this land from men who had no intentions of leaving their homes in the East to break the prairie sod or drain the prairie marshes. None of the McFarlands farmed; they owned land whose income allowed them to live in a succession of houses in Kentucky and Ohio.

This story has been passed down to us: After his marriage Eric Bergland wanted to remain in the Army Corps of Engineers and continue to survey the western territories and to work on river and harbor improvements in the south. But Lucy and her very proper and forceful mother, Mary Scott McFarland, had other ideas. And since Mary McFarland was a cousin of the wife of President Hayes, she had connections. The story goes that she used those connections to get the husband of her only daughter reassigned to tamer work at West Point and then in Baltimore, where they lived most of their married life. What Mary McFarland wanted for her only daughter was a "dear perpetual place." In a family history she wrote for her grandsons, Mary McFarland describes her first home as a young married woman, one she and her husband, John, had to leave because "at certain seasons it was malarious":

> In the suburbs of Chilicothe just beyond the toll gate going West stands a one-story brick house. It is charmingly situated on a gentle elevation commanding on one side a widely extended view of the valley of the Sciota—on another side steep and thickly wooded hills separated from the grounds by a narrow road. Two or three superb old forest trees are left standing on the lawn. . . . An Osage orange hedge planted and tended by your grandpa partially enclosed grounds beautified by choice shrubs and many rare varieties of roses. This lovely spot was our first home. A clergyman who visited us in the early summer when bud and blossom are in perfection asked if I would not feel some reluctance in exchanging this earthly Paradise for a heavenly one.

Despite her florid Victorian prose, her feeling for that place comes through, but family sympathies have always been with Major Eric Bergland and his thwarted American desire to see new territories.

We know very little about Eric and Lucy's son, our grandfather William Bergland. No one I know has a scrap of paper he wrote on. His son and daughters are not sure where he was born. This is all I know: William Berg-land grew up in Baltimore, the third son, after John and Leonard, of Eric and Lucy Bergland. He graduated from Princeton in 1908—"Aughty eight"—married Eloise Beal Bond, also from Baltimore, and moved to Wilmington, where he worked as an electrical engineer for the Dupont Company the rest of his life. He never owned a house, but he did own the farm in Illinois left to him by his parents. I remember my grandmother, then William Bergland's widow, telling me that "Berglands don't buy houses, they rent them." She said this as something she was proud of; she was telling me of a need they didn't have. Yet it is she who wrote for her younger sisters a very detailed description of her grandparents' Mount Royal house in Baltimore where she lived as a girl. The house is gone from the family, but she made sure that the memory of it is not. She described each room of the house in as much detail as she describes the library:

> There were the four windows with the lovely deep wide window sills and shutters that were unfolded and closed at night. Lace curtains and dark red ones looped back. Between the east windows was the old secretary desk with the bust of Daniel Webster on top. The floor shook so when anyone walked, or especially ran, that we were always expecting Daniel to have a great fall, but he never did.

I have said that no two generations of Berglands lived in the same place, but that is not quite true. For about fifty years there was a place that was, for the summers, a home for three generations.

In the 1890s Eric Bergland and other people from Baltimore (our other great-grandfather Hugh Lennox Bond, among them) sought a place in the north to escape the heat and malaria of Baltimore in the summer. In those days it was possible to take trains to the far north, and they did—all the way to a tiny village, North Hatley, on Lake Massawippi in southern Quebec. Eric Bergland built a house on the sloping south-facing shore of this cold northern lake, near where the river flows out, north, and eventually into the Saint Lawrence River. "It is a romantic place," and, if I were to describe it, it would sound like Anders's description of his childhood home in Sweden. The Bonds built a house next to the Berglands, and later, two of the

Bergland boys—William and Leonard—married two of the Bond girls—Eloise and Eleanor. There were many family weddings in North Hatley, and a few burials, and summer after summer of canoeing and picnics up the lake.

Most of the stories I have heard my father and his brother and sisters tell are about North Hatley. The stories have taken on the quality of family myth: This was the place where we were happy; this is the place we have lost. The houses were sold after World War II. No one could afford to keep up those big houses and economic necessity had moved the family all over the country. North Hatley is a long way from everywhere, it seems, but not so far from the place Anders named us after.

The most romantic story of connection with a place is my father's story. My father, Hugh Bergland, the middle son of five children, was born in Wilmington in 1917, around the time his grandfather Eric Bergland died. The year he graduated from Princeton with a degree in psychology was 1941, so he went almost immediately into the army. In 1944, when he was stationed at Barksdale Air Force Base in Shreveport, Louisiana, he met my mother, Elizabeth Howard, and four months later they were married. After the war, my father and mother with their infant daughter, me, went back to Wilmington to live temporarily with my father's parents while he looked for work. He wanted to teach science at a boys' boarding school. He made the rounds of schools like the one he had gone to—Middlesex—but housing was short for teachers with families, so he found no work. Then for two terms he worked for a masters in psychology at the University of Delaware, thinking that that might improve his chances of getting a teaching job. In the summer of 1946, he and my mother went up to North Hatley and stayed at the Bergland house, where, at dinner one evening, my father's Aunt Brita suggested that he think about managing the family farms out in Illinois, as Cousin Albert, the farm manager, was nearing retirement. While he had been at Princeton, my father had worked one summer on the farm in Illinois, and he had liked it out there. So, he drove out by himself to talk to Mr. Conn and Howard Burton, the farmers whose families had broken and farmed the Bergland land outside of Weldon. My father knew that if he were going to ever *manage* any farm, he had to farm, but first he had to work for farmers. Mr. Conn agreed to take my father on as a hired hand and teach him farming. When my father got back to Wilmington, my mother was ready to go west to Illinois. So in 1947 we moved to a tiny tenant house with no electricity or plumbing. After almost exactly a hundred years, there was a Bergland who was farming again. Because he loved the work, my father soon gave up the idea of managing farms, and when the older farmers retired, he took on more acres until he was farming the whole section at the time of his retirement in 1981.

That is the way he told the story to me recently. Though his reasons for living and working in Illinois were as unplanned and as much a product of the economic times as are his children's reasons for living and working where we do, we still tell a version of his story that is more romantic. We children of the sixties see Dad as the First Dropout—a man who rejected the pressures and vain pleasures of corporate life in an Eastern city and returned to the land of his fathers, a man who rejected economic security for the real and frightening economic insecurities of being a farmer. Our version embarrasses him, but that is the one we've chosen to live by.

Though we complained about the place when we were young, and although we knew at the time that selling it made economic sense, the loss of the farm in Illinois was hard for the five of us who grew up there. I will never forget driving out of the driveway that bitterly cold morning in 1982 and looking back for the last time at home—the corncribs, the bare maple trees, which were still young, the frozen yard where we'd played, and the attic window from which I had seen so much of my future arrive. I wrote my novel, *A Farm under a Lake*, largely as a way to understand that loss.

Now my parents live in Vermont, in a house that is my father's dream house in a place he had dreamed of living since he was a little boy. Every summer that my father's family took the train up to North Hatley they passed through Vermont, and my father thought that Vermont was the prettiest, most romantic place he'd ever seen. He wanted to live there. His sisters and mother accidentally made it possible for him. His eldest sister Eloise married a man who lived in Cornish, New Hampshire, and my grandmother, also Eloise, bought in the 1950s for very little money a rocky old abandoned farm across the river in Vermont so she could be near her daughter. It is a beautiful site, but the land is so poor and the old house so cold that the old man who grew up in it recently said he never wanted to see that cold place again. "It is a romantic place." When my Aunt Lucy inherited the farm, she divided the land, giving my father and Aunt Eloise parcels to build on.

My parents' house was built in 1976, but it feels like an old home. My sister and I were both married there, my brother Bond's baby was born there, and we recently celebrated our parents' fiftieth wedding anniversary there.

I know that this new place in Vermont has kept alive the idea of a "dear perpetual place" in my family. And the place is very beautiful. Except for Hukna Lake, this place too sounds like Anders's farm. And it was our favorite romantic place to go as children. From the hill that is my parents' rocky front yard, you look east across the Connecticut River, invisible in the valley, to the White Mountains of New Hampshire, mountains that are almost always blue—sometimes a blue as heavy as granite, but more often a blue as insubstantial as a Japanese watercolor. Or, disappearing behind rising mists, they are as thin as memories of mountains. They are the blue of forgetting.

A few weeks ago, my brother John Bergland, who lives in Oregon, came here to Milwaukee to travel with me out to Vermont for our parents' fiftieth wedding anniversary celebration. Before we left for the airport, we went for a walk in a park near my home, a park on the Milwaukee River. As we walked, and secretly glanced at each other's surprisingly gray hair, we talked about the future, about where we wanted to be when we are old. We talked about how nice it would be to live near each other again, with the others, in a place where all the children could come and take root too. But then he began to tell me of his lifelong dream to travel in tropical places, to live in Mexico, and I told him of my desire to see stark northern places, and we talked of his two older children, who are establishing themselves in Seattle, and of our brother Bond, who has recently moved from New York to San Francisco. So we gave up on that "dear perpetual place" train of thought because we're old enough to know how little we can make happen by dreaming, or even planning. Especially when all our dreams conflict. We'll wait and see.

And as we walked, we looked around. It was late afternoon. The sky was an aching blue. There were no clouds. It was cool. The light was that clear and bright and yellow light that you know is not local light, but belongs to all the earth, or anyway all the earth at this latitude, on this continent. Here in this park was all we dreamed of as children, not as grandiose, but it was all here: paths that disappeared into dark woods, old willow trees beside a winding river, a waterfall—all of this planned and made by romantic and civic people.

What was happening all around us was the great slow ceremony of autumn in North America.

We walked past some hawthorns and crab apples, which looked like plain bridesmaids, up a little rise into an oak wood still green and dark, but beyond the dark trunks of the great trees we could see the pure gold and the purple-bronze of the ash trees. And then we walked beside the river on a beaten-down path where you have to climb over the gnarled roots of the silver maples that lean out over the water, sheltering the blue heron. Then, ducking under a red fringe of sumac, we turned away from the river with its attendant geese and headed back to the car on a path mowed through a prairie that pressed on us all the smells and colors and sounds we could ever wish for.

And then it seemed that *this* was where I would always want to be. How could I ever want another place? Why would I ever have to *own* a place? All lands are public lands and we write to be stewards of memory.

Remembering Houses

Jon Hassler

From the dining-room window of the Wilson house at the north edge of town, I could look uphill past the creek to Jonnie Read's house. Jonnie Read was my first friend. It seemed fitting that we should be friends, since he spelled his first name the way I did, without the unnecessary *h*. His birthday party was my first social occasion. My eager anticipation turned into anxiety when I discovered his house full of three- and four-year-olds I'd never seen before. From the corners of rooms, I meekly watched them screaming, wrestling, bursting balloons, and gorging themselves on popcorn and cake. Where did all these strangers come from, and why was Jonnie Read paying them more attention than he paid me? I cried. Mrs. Read called my mother, who came and took me home.

But this party is not my earliest memory. Riding over the snow on a sled was the first event in my life I remember. My father had equipped the sled with a box to contain me and my blankets, and my mother and I were making our way downtown through a gray afternoon to visit him at work. We passed the houses of Margie, Frankie, Billy, Sammy, and Nancy—children

Copyright 1995 by Jon Hassler

whose existence I was not yet aware of, and whose birthday parties, alas, I was destined to attend.

Next I remember being read to in a rocking chair by my cousin Bunny, who came from Montana and lived with us during her high-school years, and then by my mother's aunt Elizabeth, a teacher who stayed with us during her summer vacations. I loved both of these women, but not equally, because Aunt Elizabeth made inflexible demands concerning my table manners.

Next I remember my first haircut. I vomited on the barber out of fear because, scissors in hand, he came at me wearing a white smock and I thought he was a doctor about to cut me.

When the Depression deepened and house rent ($22.50 per month) proved too extravagant for us, we moved to the Nichols apartments half a block off Main Street. Here we had access to a wide upstairs porch from which we could see the store where my father worked, the post office where my mother seemed to derive a lot of pleasure sending and receiving letters, the church where we went to mass, and the public school where I was compelled to attend kindergarten. From my bedroom window I looked down on Bob Batcher's oil station and experienced my first vocational aspiration. I wanted to become a fuel oil deliverer and drive a blue Pure Oil truck like Bob Batcher's.

In the next apartment lived Mrs. Demarais, a kindly widow who smelled of garlic and with whom I sometimes stayed when my parents were away. Downstairs lived a railroader named Elmer Johnson who hated to be awakened before noon on his days off. When I was five my parents bought a piano with a view toward making a musician of me. The piano was too large for our rooms, so we kept it in the foyer downstairs. As I was practicing my scales one Sunday morning, Elmer Johnson came raging out of his apartment and chased me up the steps calling me a goddamn twerp. After that, I had to practice on an improvised keyboard my father made out of cardboard, with adhesive tape for the white keys, electrician's tape for the black. The fact that I never became a concert pianist I blame on Elmer Johnson and the discouraging effect of playing scales on that strip of soundless cardboard.

I started kindergarten three days late because I had chicken pox. My mother took me to the door of the classroom, pointed out Jonnie Read and other children milling about at the far end of a long room, and kissed me good-bye. I was horrified to think of leaving her for the rest of the morning, but I held back my tears and stepped through the door into eighteen years of education. I was halfway down the room when two boys came at me with a pair of dime-store handcuffs, and they led me, manacled and terrified, over to a dark closet and closed me inside. I've come to think of that event as emblematic of my schooling. From that point through graduate school, with very few exceptions, I never entered a classroom with anything but the heavy heart of a prisoner, dreading the hour of stultifying tedium that lay ahead.

The day after Hitler invaded Poland, I entered first grade. Sister Simona taught me the Apostles' Creed, Ramona Overby wrote me love notes, and Leo Kowalski—whenever Sister was out of the room—displayed his penis. In second grade (same room, same teacher) my classmate Billy Burke told me he'd quit smoking. In third grade, we studied under Sister Constance, going deeper into theology. Why did your guardian angel insist on remaining invisible? In fasting from solid foods, could you have a thin milkshake?

In third grade our pastor presented each of us with an apple on his name's day (December 6, the Feast of St. Nicholas). I took my apple home and forgot it, and when, weeks later, I found it black and rotten at the back of the refrigerator, I believed I was guilty of a sacrilege too serious to be forgiven. I might have consulted my confessor if he weren't the same man who'd given out the apples and therefore would surely be grieved to know how careless I'd been with his gift.

I was a champion believer. With only one exception, I believed every fact, myth, and holy opinion taught me during those four years of parochial school. I believed in the Communion of Saints, the Knights of Columbus, the multiplication tables, and life everlasting. I believed in the efficacy of prayer, fasting, phonics, scrap metal drives, and war bonds. The one thing I had trouble believing in was Sister Constance's prohibition of the word *leg*. She said we must always say "limb" because "leg" had improper connotations. I never believed that.

By this time we'd moved out of the Nichols apartments and into the Loso house, where we lived from my sixth to my ninth year. (Houses in small towns bear the names of their original or previous owners.) Here again we had wide and pleasing views from the upstairs windows. From my bedroom, I could look down on Billy Shelver's house across the alley. I've never been especially aggressive, but once in my life I felt the fierce animal pleasure of overpowering someone weaker than myself and giving him a bloody nose. It was Billy Shelver's nose. Billy was a year younger than I. Reenacting Pearl Harbor in the alley with our toy soldiers and airplanes, Billy had the audacity to utter the word *weapons*. It was a word unfamiliar to me, so I beat him up.

Nor had I developed any grace where birthday parties were concerned. I went to Richie Barret's sixth birthday party with the most wonderful gift I could imagine, a windup motorcycle with a sidecar. I also went with a full bladder. Too timid to ask where the bathroom was, I prowled alone through the Barrets' large house, and halfway upstairs I paused on the landing to water a houseplant, and then I hurried home with the motorcycle because I couldn't bear to part with it.

In the Loso house I had a dog. His name was Jippie. I didn't often require a confidant, for as an only child I'd learned the art of conversing with myself, but on those special occasions when I needed to say private things out loud, Jippie was my listener. He was a mixed-blood terrier, white with black spots. He barked only at a certain few people, not everyone, who walked past our house. He took a particular dislike to Mr. Davenport, who used to mutter insults at him on his way downtown. Maybe it was Mr. Davenport who fed him ground glass and brought about his agonizing death in the shade of the lilac bush in our backyard. While my father dug Jippie's grave and buried him, I stayed on the opposite side of the house, playing catch with myself by throwing a tennis ball against the wall. It took him a long time because the earth was dry and hard that summer. I didn't stop playing catch until I heard him put the shovel in the garage and start the car to go to work.

My father's work was that of a grocer. Until I was nine, he managed a chain store for the Red Owl Company. Red Owl promised him a new and larger store down the street, in a building being put up by a local contractor, but Red Owl reneged at the last minute and allowed my father's competitor, National Tea, to take it over. So my father, vexed, quit Red Owl, and we moved to Minneapolis, the city of my birth, where he got a job in a war plant that manufactured grease guns for military vehicles. We moved in with my mother's parents on Aldrich Avenue South.

This house was a block and a half from Clara Barton school, where I found that none of my fourth-grade classmates lived near me. No matter. I was content to while away my afternoons and evenings in solitary pleasures like reading comic books, collecting stamps, and prowling about the house and yard pretending I was a fighter pilot shot down behind enemy lines and sneaking back to safety. One very cold day in January, as I tunneled through a hardpacked snowdrift, progressing inch by inch across Norway and back to my outfit, I broke through into daylight and discovered myself being spied upon by a twelve-year-old boy I'd seen in the neighborhood but never spoken to. His odd first name was Harlow. To my great disappointment, he asked if we could be friends. I sensed what sort of overbearing friend he'd turn out to be; nevertheless I said okay because to decline would have been impolite, and immediately we took up our roles as lord and servant. To this day, if Harlow remembers me, he probably thinks I liked him, for I was a master of cowardly deceit.

Fourth grade was Eskimos, long division, and Miss Bullard. Despite Miss Bullard's solicitude, or maybe because of it, I couldn't seem to shake my distress over living in a city where the likes of Harlow was the best and only friend a fellow could find, and where the classroom walls were bereft of the consoling images of the Sacred Heart and the Blessed Virgin and various other saints and martyrs. I myself played the saint and martyr, displaying my unhappiness in order to attract Miss Bullard's continued attention.

Let the Sunday I cut my thumb stand for my perfidious behavior as a city boy. Harlow was forever building things out of the scrap lumber in his basement. This Sunday we were building bazookas designed after those we saw in the newsreels. My part was to hold the boards and dowels as Harlow used the handsaw. The saw jumped and cut my thumb to the bone. Bleeding and screaming, I ran home to my parents and grandparents, where I was duly fussed over and bandaged and (what a relief!) forbidden to play in Harlow's basement anymore. Next morning in school, Miss Bullard excused me from the long-division quiz because of my bandaged thumb. As the others worked, she came to my desk and consulted with me in whispers. "And what was it you were building?" she asked.

I didn't answer. I hated to tell her a bazooka. She struck me as too tender hearted to receive the news with equanimity that I was manufacturing weapons of violence. Surely it would remove me from the role I was playing as her innocent pet.

"A birdhouse?" she prompted.

"Yes, a birdhouse," I lied, shielding her from the awful truth.

We were in the city less than a full year when my parents decided to buy a grocery store of their own. Consulting with the Red Owl people, they found that the only one they could afford was a squalid little business situated on a short Main Street a hundred miles south of Minneapolis. How such an unpromising store could excite their enthusiasm was a mystery to me, but of course I said nothing cautionary or discouraging because I was being liberated from the city of my discontent.

Over the next eight years, happily enslaved by their dream, my parents built themselves a thriving trade, selling groceries in the postwar farming boom, and I enjoyed what I've come to think of as the idyllic segment of my life.

Our first residence in this village was the Leahy house at the edge of town, a tall clapboard structure with a cornfield rustling up against the back porch and the stockyards across the street. Miss Leahy herself, a humorless old maid, lived upstairs, while we occupied the ground floor, where mice ate the fringes off our rugs. A family of rabbits lived in the basement and ate the squash my parents stored there.

Next door, in a low house beyond a small field of cabbage, lived the Schreibers. Besides cabbage, the Schreibers raised chickens, pigeons, and two sons named Irvin and Adolf. Mr. Schreiber, who worked at the feed mill, would gladly spring a nail out of his ear whenever you asked. The younger son, near my age and surely the last American ever to be christened Adolf, asked him to demonstrate for me on their back stoop. "Show Jon the nail trick, Dad." Whereupon his father put the head end of a large nail into his left ear. We stood close and watched it go half an inch deeper as he pressed on the point; then he lifted away his finger and the nail flew out of his ear and landed in the dirt ten feet away.

Their back stoop was also where Mrs. Schreiber, a jolly, heavy woman, killed chickens. Although I witnessed this butchery a dozen times, the first time was unequaled for excitement. "Watch, she'll throw the hatchet," Adolf whispered to me as his mother laid the motionless bird on the stoop, her left hand tightly gripping its legs. With an unblinking eye, the chicken watched her raise the hatchet and bring it down—chop!—and then as it began its death spasm, she threw the bird up and away from her, involuntarily throwing the hatchet as well. Lifting herself to her feet and retrieving the hatchet, she turned her back on the headless bird, which went speeding crookedly down the dirt driveway, spurting blood. It tipped over in the tall grass beside the road and fluttered and scratched its way into a small cement culvert and lay still. I was awestruck. Adolf was in stitches. "Don't tell Ma," he whispered.

"Where did it go?" she asked, looking around.

Adolf couldn't contain his delight. He jigged about, doubled over with giggles.

"Now you boys listen here," she said angrily. "A chicken don't disappear into the ground."

I pretended to search among the cabbages.

"Adolf, you seen the chicken go—I'll take the strap to you."

His response was a screech of laughter, so she scurried into the house and came out with a razor strap that dragged on the ground. I watched the struggle from the cabbage patch. She gripped Adolf by the arm and tried to whip him but he wouldn't stand still. He ran in a circle, turning her around, and the strap, on which she had taken too long a hold, waved in a loop and never caught up with her aim. Instead of increasing her anger, this obviously struck her as humorous, for she began to laugh, and soon they were both laughing so hard they could barely stand.

"Okay," said Adolf breathlessly, pretending to confess. "It went under the house." This settled the matter, for their tiny house was supported at the corners by cement blocks, and the space underneath was too narrow for crawling, the ground too uneven for probing with a stick. Giving up on that roasting hen, Mrs. Schreiber waddled off to the chicken coop for another. Adolf went into the house and came out with an armload of comic books.

On our way to the stockyards to read them, I asked what would happen to the missing chicken. "Won't you tell her where it is?"

"Naw, let the crows and foxes have it—we got lots of chickens. My ma's never any good with the strap. Is yours?"

"We don't have a strap," I told him.

Adolf looked amazed.

The stalls and corrals of the stockyards were empty of stock, as usual. The gates, if you put your weight on the bottom board as you opened them, squealed like pigs. We sat hidden in a cattle chute and rolled a cigarette made of newspaper and dry alfalfa and then lay back to read about Captain Marvel, Mutt and Jeff, and the Katzenjammer Kids. The wind singing in the knots and cracks of the weathered boards sounded like whining cats.

Most of the friends I was making in grade five—Turk, Babe, Kenny, Dale, and Bob—lived near one another on the opposite end of town from the Leahy house, and so it seemed like blessed providence when my parents chose to buy a house in their midst. This was the Anding house, a bungalow on an elm-shaded lot ample enough for gardens, picnics, a croquet court, and pickup football games.

Football became my obsession. Basketball and baseball came and went with the seasons, but football we played through the heat of summer and in snowdrifts up to our thighs. When night fell, we devised a game limited to the area of the backyard lit by our patio lamppost, a form of football played entirely on our knees.

Eventually I came to know the ecstasy of high-school football. Across the street from our house lay the athletic field, newly landscaped and equipped with banks of lights on new steel towers.

"My blood is in those towers," my father was fond of saying, and it was true. In a remarkable effort of community cooperation, the local merchants, my father among them, made monthly trips to Rochester to sell their blood for twenty dollars a pint and thus pay for the lights and towers.

My specialty was tackling. I didn't have much of a throwing arm, or enough leg strength to be a runner, or enough bulk to play defensive lineman, but I did have the speed and fearlessness of a linebacker. In my maroon-and-gold uniform, number 38, I went up against all the ball handlers from Lewiston, Wabasha, Cannon Falls, Lake City, Stewartville, St. Felix, Dodge Center, and our archrival, St. Charles—and I knocked every one of them off his pins. Twenty-seven years later, when the first bound copy of my first novel arrived in the mail, the gratifying thrill was not unprecedented in my life. It was a thrill as great as, but no greater than, the satisfaction I felt in October 1950, the night we beat St. Charles 49–0, on our way to the Whitewater League championship.

Here the grocery store intrudes more and more on my consciousness and replaces my memory of houses. I see myself in the Red Owl trimming lettuce, candling eggs, stocking shelves. I see the villagers passing along the checkout counter like the cast of characters they turned out to be, for I later wrote a novel about this village in the corn. I see Mrs. Higgins, for example, asking me for a pound of Harvest Queen coffee, and I see myself take a bag off the shelf and straighten out the two metal ears that seal it, and I open the hopper at the top of the grinder and flick on the power switch and turn the dial to drip because Mrs Higgins always takes drip. I tip the pound of beans into the hopper and hold the bag under the chute, and after ten seconds of raucous grinding the blades whine as they run free, and my nose itches with coffee chaff as I switch off the power. It's a minute or more, then, before the coffee smell recedes to the level of the celery smell, potato smell, vinegar smell, Fig Newton smell, sausage smell, and all the rest of the pleasing smells I grew up with.

And here, because of that novel, my memories grow unreliable. I can no longer be absolutely certain whether I'm remembering scenes from my life or from my book. In a successful novel, fact and imagination must blend as subtly as the smells in this store of ours. Before the reader opens the book, each of the sixty characters, each of the five thousand images, must be fit-ted into place, ready to contribute to the pleasing effect of a good read—just as, when you unlock the store in the morning and step inside, the perfect balance of all these innumerable smells indicates that every item is in its place and doing its part to make this a seemly enterprise. Smelling potatoes over everything else means a rotten potato somewhere, and if you're hit with a whiff of vinegar it means a leaky barrel. It's the perfectly balanced mix that tells you all is well.

Breckenridge Hills, 63114

David Haynes

From twenty feet over our heads a bug-encrusted fixture cast a pool of yellowish light onto the corner outside my parents' bungalow. In the summer after the ice-cream man had come and the mosquito fog truck had passed with its cloud of appealingly sweet poison, the kids in the neighborhood gathered at the standard for a game of hide-and-seek. The good hiding places were just the other side of a privacy hedge Mr. Granberry had planted and also within the thick branches of the forsythia bush on the other side of the driveway where my father parked his Buick. I was a base-sticker—not the brave kind like my sister, who would hover behind whoever was "it" and run in before he could call "one-two-three on Kim." I made myself quiet inside and stood just beyond the circle of light where everything was shadows and variations of black, and where a shape could be a branch or a dog or a whole clutch of kids. I would imagine I couldn't be seen.

I was a base-sticker because I was afraid that if I hid no one would come looking for me. I had my reasons. It had happened to me before, now and then. While "it" sang the song about robins and rolling pins, I would tiptoe

Copyright 1995 by David Haynes

away and stoop behind Mr. Hayden's upholstery truck or around behind the playground fence that was tangled with honeysuckle. I would hear the others yelling "safe" or hear them being caught. Then I would hear the new "it" start the song again. "Last night, night before / Twenty-four robins at my door." I would still be hiding. Forgotten. No one had even bothered looking for me.

This is not about self-pity. (Well, maybe a little.) For the most part I didn't mind not being caught. It was better than having to sing that stupid song and chase people around in the dark. I believed I had outsmarted them all, you see: that I knew the best hiding places, that I would win forever. I would freeze in my place and wait and listen. At my most daring I fantasized someone else would find me. Some other kids from some other game. Some mysterious stranger. Someone I liked better than the kids in the game.

I was not the kid in the neighborhood everyone loved. I was, instead, the "smart kid." People do not love the smart kid. They gape at the smart kid. They put up with him. They pet him and ask him inane questions and for the recitation of facts. My specialty was geography. I could name the capitals of all fifty states and most foreign countries. I knew the names of obscure rivers and lakes and the chief agricultural and industrial products of Ohio. I knew what the Piedmont was. Such information might get you out of Breckenridge Hills, but it didn't necessarily make you popular.

In my hiding place I made mental maps of the neighborhood and imagined where the others hid. I could hear them breathing and whispering and knew exactly who was behind my father's rose bushes and who had climbed the Chinese elm and who was flush against the floor of the playground shed. I knew just where to look should I ever become "it."

I was smart and I was also naive. It was a long time before I figured out that they never found me because they didn't care to. I'd be lying if I said I was crushed. In a neighborhood where such virtues as fast legs for running, a good hoop shot, and a mouth full of snappy and vulgar wit were valued—items missing from my personal repertoire—I was long past caring what Mark and Charles and Valerie and the other kids I played with thought about me. I played with them, I think, out of habit, because it was an excuse to stay out after the fireflies emerged, because I was supposed to, because I didn't know any better. Inside I kept hoping the real friends that I was meant to have in the world would show up. Some other kids who would come and find me and in some way change my world. Those other kids: the ones who cared about books and ideas and about the many different kinds of people they have over there in India. I had no doubt those real friends would come. In the meantime I waited in my hiding place. Eventually I became bolder and moved into the shadows of light just beyond the heart of the game, pacing closer, amazed at how, despite everything I knew—all the atlases and world's worth of useless trivia—I had somehow learned how not to be seen.

Breckenridge Hills you will not find on very many maps. I don't believe I actually saw the name written down until I was almost an adult and someone happened to point out the city limits sign. It was in the context of a joke. The only person I knew who referred to where we lived as Breckenridge Hills was my mother. She liked the vaguely country-clubby, pseudo chichi sound of the name, and it particularly stuck in her craw that even if we lived in some sort of quasi-suburban governmental entity by that name, Breckenridge Hills was, in fact, not our mailing address. The post office was in Overland. Most people who sent us Christmas cards preferred to write the eight letters instead of the seventeen.

Saint Louis County, Missouri, was at one time balkanized into a patchwork of hundreds of jurisdictions, surviving from the days when any collection of taverns and feed stores gave itself a name so that people knew where their wagons had stopped. Velda Village. Des Peres. Saint John. Spanish Lake. Many have disappeared, swallowed up by more affluent or successful neighbors. Not Breckenridge Hills. Recently, my father announced to me with a certain amount of pride that Breckenridge Hills had been upgraded from a village to city. You'd have to have spent time there to appreciate the irony.

I find it hard to describe Breckenridge Hills. I want to give you a picture in your head, to apply a metaphor—to say that Breckenridge Hills is like— but in the collective sum of metaphors and analogies and examples, mined from the depths of literature and pop culture, there are no places like Breck-enridge Hills. When I watched *Leave It to Beaver* and *My Three Sons* and *Bewitched* I would have a feeling that I now know is some kind of disso-nance. I would watch the cars coursing up and down the streets on *Dragnet* and *Adam 12* and never quite be able to enjoy the story but for the sense that there was something wrong with the picture. Where those people lived didn't look anything like our neighborhood. I was besieged on my first trip to California by memories of streets I had seen only in black and white and yet seemed more familiar to me than home. I have never seen a represen-tation of a place like Breckenridge Hills. It is important to me to figure out how to talk about it.

The houses on our cul-de-sac had been built in the heart of what had been an orchard. Behind our house stood a row of ancient "plum" trees. I put plum in quotation marks because I have looked through supermarkets and vegetable stands across this country and never seen any fruit that even vaguely resembles these "plums." Our plums were the size of a large cherry, but, when ripe, a brighter and more shocking red color with sometimes swirls of yellow mixed in. The somewhat tough skin contained school-bus orange flesh the texture of an overripe peach. They peaked in late August into what for me was a sickeningly sweet mush that the birds and squirrels loved. I hated those plums. The middle of three children and, therefore, the designated lawn-mower slave, I refused to rake them up before I did my chore and dreaded pushing along behind the smoky, oil-encrusted antique my father insisted didn't merit replacing and feeling their ooze spread from beneath my tennis shoes. The smell of the rotten brown goo cooking up in the sun has been enough to make me think twice about anything in the plum family to this day.

The other kids in the neighborhood, of course, loved the fresh fruit. Philistines. I personally could never understand how they put the crap in their mouths.

"Can we come in your yard and get some cherries?" they would ask. They called them cherries. I would shrug. It wasn't up to me. My mother, you see, did not allow "loitering in her yard." She preferred not to have "those heathens eat up all her fruit." Don't get the wrong idea: I don't think in my entire life I saw my mother eat one of those plums. Neither did she stew them up for dessert or make preserves. Her prohibition, in fact, was not about the fruit at all—the key words above being *heathen* and *loitering*. She'd just as soon not have "those people" in her presence, thank you very much. My brother and sister, more the rebels than I, brazenly escorted whoever expressed interest back to the orchard for a feeding frenzy. Mother reserved the sort of fit for this transgression one imagines temperamental actresses having behind the scenes on soap operas. It was ugly: mother scolding and hectoring and my siblings howling with laughter.

Me? I would have been standing in the front yard examining the caterpillars on the elm tree, or flat on my back on the enameled metal glider in our side yard, staring into the blue sky at the kaleidoscopes created by my vision.

"David," some kid would call from the street. "Why your mother won't let us eat no cherries?"

I ignored them. Despite wishing they would pick the damn trees clean it never occurred to me to tell them to help themselves. As if plums were important. As if I cared.

The main reason I have trouble talking to you about Breckenridge Hills is that I am far from ambivalent about it. I have strong feelings. I hate it a lot. I also feel something that is close to the opposite of hate, though love is surely the wrong word. *Like* is also wrong and so it would also be wrong to say I have a fondness for the Hills. A combination of understanding and affection is about as close as I can get.

I know Breckenridge Hills. That seems a fair statement. And though it is changing, it is pretty much the place in my memories. In some ways I feel like the only witness to a horrible disaster, or the historian who has dedicated his life to the details of some murderous battle of the American Civil War. There's pride, but there's some shame mixed in, as well. Why would one want to be such an expert? What if no one cares?

When friends talk of growing up in your garden variety suburb of Anyplace, U.S.A., they could be talking about Breckenridge Hills. Yes, it has quiet, tree-lined streets and carbon-copy track homes and, yes, you may apply your stereotypes of such environments to our little village and in many ways they would be accurate. Like all stereotypes they are both true and untrue.

The truth: most of Breckenridge Hills was pretty trashy. It is also true that the black part was far from the trashiest area, and in many ways set the standard for lawn care and cleanliness. The street maintenance crew lived in the black area. We never had potholes and our street was the first one plowed on the rare snow day.

The white part of the Hills had more than its share of folks recently transplanted from the rural south. They have this thing down there about old appliances in the front yard and cars up on blocks. They were what we called poor white trash.

None of us—black or white—was too rich. We were working-class people—factory workers, postmen, auto body repair people like my father. Everyone had a job, and in the mornings you could hear all the cars start up just after dawn, rolling off to the salt mines. Just like your garden variety suburb.

Though it really wasn't that way at all.

Rich black folks lived in other places, like down in the city or in University City. My parents knew some of them. Some had moved from Breckenridge Hills when they'd gotten a little more money, but not many, really. The Hills was the sort of place you got there and you stayed

We have erased working-class places and people from our culture. Only *Roseanne* dares show them with any clarity. The Connors could have been the parents of any number of friends of mine. But where are the black faces, and where are places like this where brown faces play in the street at night without the fear of evil? Why wasn't this story ever told, and what happens if it disappears?

Some years we walked to Marvin School and some years we were bused. Sometimes it was explained that we were more than a mile from school and were therefore eligible to be bused. Sometimes it was explained that we were less than a mile from school and therefore had to walk. Sometimes there was no explanation: the rule just changed. This is what a lot of childhood is like—having the rules change for arbitrary and illogical reasons and being expected to pretend your brain is too undeveloped to notice. Children are gracious: They play along. Adults have ways of dealing with those who don't.

I preferred the walking years. Our school sat high above the corner of Saint Charles Rock Road and Woodson Road—two busy and well-traveled thoroughfares in northwest Saint Louis County. When the bell rang at the end of the school day, all the kids from Breckenridge Hills would barrel down a crumbly old concrete staircase. When a sufficient number of us had gathered, the police patrol would stop traffic in all four directions and signal us to make the diagonal run to the quadrant where our houses were. The implication was clear: You dawdled and he was letting the traffic go. You would be flattened! I liked to pretend I was one of the Israelites heading home from years of bad luck in Egypt. The pharaohs were those loser kids who did not make the first mad dash for the first crossing to the Hills. We would run across that street and scream and many days I swear I could feel on my legs the hot exhaust of the first cars closing the portal behind me.

There were many ways to get to our part of Breckenridge Hills. One could walk down Woodson Road or one could walk down the Rock Road. There were good streets to walk on—like Marvin Avenue and Breckenridge Road and Quiet Lane—and there were a number of streets we were told not to walk on. Calvert and Dix Avenues in particular were rumored to harbor virulent racists with shotguns and pit bulls.

I liked to walk down Woodson and take the "shortcut" through a rubbish-strewn vacant lot to Marvin Avenue. I had many friends and fans on the way home. There was a white girl who lived on the way who always had a house full of cats. Each week a new litter arrived and she tried to foist one off on me. I always took one and was always ordered to return it the next day. That girl was the first person I ever met who lived in a garbage house. I was not supposed to go in there, but I could see from the door that with the exception of the paths they used to go from room to room, the house was packed floor to ceiling with garbage. A large part of me was grossed out. Another large part of me was fascinated. It took a lot of nerve to live like that. Seeing it had proved to me that despite my father's admonitions to the contrary, one could live life surrounded by filth, and that dusting and vacuuming were, more than anything else, affectations.

There were a couple of old ladies who made a habit of greeting me on my way home. A couple of white ladies and some black ones. They would be standing in their yards doing old lady things like gardening or sweeping the walk. I have an image of myself walking up and down the streets, waving and smiling as if I were a beauty pageant candidate on a runway. I have no recollection of talking to these women about anything. Also, on the way home was what I later learned was an Osage orange tree. Osage oranges bear grapefruit-sized green pods that resemble round brains. We called it the brain tree. The first time I noticed them I froze in horror. I didn't understand how nature could produce something so repellent. For a long time I walked on the other side of the street to avoid them. Later, after I got used to the strange green balls, I developed the idea that this particular tree—not the species, but the very tree on the corner of Breckenridge and Calvert—was a unique mutant being that did not exist elsewhere on earth. I also believed it was important to not cross the street, but to walk right by it, right underneath it. It was important to cultivate relationships with things such as this tree—things that were so incredibly wrong and out of place. The only time I avoided it was during the fall when the seed pods rotted and fell to the ground: one did not want to walk through green brain pulp. A lot of my childhood I spent worrying about stepping in things.

Brave boys took another shortcut. A path hugged the edge of a gully above the creek that ran between Breckenridge Road and Marvin Avenue. Coldwater Creek was, in fact, a countywide system of storm sewers, designed to shunt rainwater to the Mississippi River. In the places where the rich people lived, the sides were paved in concrete and the lip of the ravine planted in decorative shrubbery. In Breckenridge Hills we had eroded embankments and old tires and weeds. Water: well, here and there you could find a stagnant pool of some kind. You could find crawdads, too, if you knew where to look and you had enough guts to get down there and wallow around. When it rained the creek turned into a torrent. People had been washed away. I was not allowed to take the creek path.

One day in second grade I did. I followed some sixth-graders down the path. It seemed like a big adventure—like something out of a Tarzan movie. Everything would have been fine except I got stuck on a piece of barbed wire. Stuck really good, too. Despite what I did, I could not undo my sweater.

I panicked. I cried a little and I yelled for somebody to help me. Then I stopped all that. I decided it was vulgar and ridiculous to be having a big fit about being pinned to a fence. Someone would come along and get me out. I was less than fifty feet from civilization—albeit a rather tacky and grubby one. I quelled my usual worries about pythons, poison ivy, and tetanus and settled in for the wait. I was a very stoical child.

Eventually (probably about five minutes later) I was rescued by some white boys—the same ones I had followed in the first place. They insisted on walking me all the way to my house and making sure I got home okay. Sweet and responsible of them, but I spent most of the trip making up stories like a cornered bank robber in an attempt to ditch them. It didn't work. They delivered me to the front door as dutifully as the postman delivers rejected manuscripts. Mother thanked them profusely and sent them on their way.

Then she set about embellishing the truth.

I had gotten lost. I had been lured into the woods. I had been trapped for hours. I had been disoriented, unable to find my way home. Thank God for those boys!

One of the reasons I became a writer is that I have never gotten over the fact that my mother completely missed the point of this story. She had made me into the victim and into the butt of the joke. She'd trot out this old saw on any and every occasion for years: she remembers it to this day, and she tells it and smiles in a way that is less affectionate than spiteful.

Forget the niggling matter that my experience and her story existed in two alternative universes. She could make up all the crap about me she wanted—I couldn't have cared less—as long as I could at least find myself in there somewhere, but I never could: I was never the helpless butterball of her fiction. But I am begging the question.

Think back, Mother. Find the real heart of the tale. Before the heroes, the escort, before the torn sweater, before the fence even.

It's the fork in the road that matters. The point I chose the other path in the first place.

I imagine, deep in her heart, she knew that.

Most of the houses the black people lived in in Breckenridge Hills were built between 1947 and 1949 by a builder named Vatterott. Each house was pretty much identical. A living room–dining room combination. A kitchen. A "utility" room. Two bedrooms and a bath. Most of those utility rooms became third bedrooms down the line.

When I went to high school and made friends with some white kids, I found out that most of them had grown up in Vatterott homes too. We would go over to each other's houses and find out we already knew where everything was. Our big joke was that after the bomb there would be three things left: cockroaches, crabgrass, and Vatterott homes.

In the black part of Breckenridge Hills many people were related to the Carter or the Hollins family. Everyone had a lot of kids—my parents' three being an exceptionally small number. I was among the youngest. My brother—two years older than me—was one of the first black kids to ever go all the way through Ritenour schools. Most of the older kids had gone to segregated Elmwood school—about ten miles away—and then to high school in the city.

Though only ten years or so older, those kids had very different lives from us younger ones. They had become stars at city high schools with names like Vashon and Soldan and Beaumont. Black schools. They had complicated relationships with their peers and with their parents and with a variety of exotic adults. Two girls were rumored to have had babies with members of various professional sports franchises. One man we knew had been followed home from Vietnam by a woman who wheeled his baby up and down the street at various odd hours. She disappeared a while ago. No one knows to where.

Of those of us born since '52, no one knows quite where we fit in the scheme. A few years ago, at my brother's funeral, a number of these older kids—many now grandparents—approached me to express their sympathies. A common question was how soon I would be graduating from college.

I was thirty-five.

Fun facts to know and tell: Chuck Berry's brother lived one block over from us. Ike Turner's brother lived on the corner at the bottom of the hill. Three houses up from Ike's brother lived the brother of baseball star Bob Gibson.

More fun facts: My parents' house payment was thirty-five dollars a month.

A lot of this is in the past tense. You can change most of it to present. Very few of us left. Most of the people are still there. And their children. And now their grandchildren. Most of it is still true. The Vatterott homes have taken on dignity beneath the mature trees that surround them.

As far as the rest of the Hills: Except for two Cub Scout den mothers and the girl with the cats, I never knew any of the people who lived in the white part of Breckenridge Hills.

My creative life was nurtured by a place that was both segregated and integrated. Both black and white, far from rich but nothing like poor either. Everyone watched television, voted Democratic, ate fatty foods. The nearest library was two miles away.

More important: My creative life was nurtured in a place that was, more than anything else, a joke. Being working class has always been a big joke in this country. (As if working yourself to death was funny.) Being working class and black is like a joke told in a language you don't speak: You know you're supposed to laugh but you don't quite know why.

I was the sort of child who read the Brontës and Ellison and Bradbury and Dickens. I also love Kmart and those long drags of suburban road lined by one discount strip mall after the other. My childhood wardrobe came from Robert Hall. I love that we have a president who knows what a good chimichanga is.

No one has expectations of the working class except that we work. I don't recall ever studying for a class or having to work particularly hard for a grade. Most of school seemed superfluous to my life. I only knew there were hoops to be jumped through in order to get on to college or on to someplace else. A working-class black kid in a third-rate suburban nowhere: I had no idea where someplace else was. I still don't know. I just knew it was desirable and I was supposed to get there. I imagined it looked like the place where the Beaver and My Three Sons lived.

In St. Louis there is only one main marker of your social status: "Where did you go to high school?" I won't honor those institutions whose names are the correct answer to the question. You all know who you are.

My answer was one of the wrong ones.

I went to Ritenour.

Satisfied?

Ritenour. What can I tell you about Ritenour, except it is the kind of high school most people believe working-class kids deserve. It was the kind of high school where the counselors had scripts tacked to the walls of their cubicles containing sentences such as "Can I interest you in the technical school?" When I got admitted to Macalester College in St. Paul, I remember a counselor calling me down to make sure there was in fact a student by my name and that some mistake had not been made.

There were 960 people in my high-school graduating class. Ten of us were black. Race was far from the most perplexing thing about Ritenour.

When students from Ritenour show up to take their SATs, other students roll their eyes and laugh.

Newscasters always mispronounce Ritenour because it is the sort of place they try to avoid mentioning.

I could go on, including a whole series of jokes (such as the reason Ritenour plays football only on Saturday afternoon is that on Friday night they need a place for the cheerleaders to graze). The point is, even now when I tell people who are familiar with St. Louis where I went to high school, they back away. Scholars. Politicians. Writers. People who should know better.

The students at my alma mater have recently had new sweatshirts printed up. They have expropriated the logo of the television series *Beverly Hills, 90210* and replaced the name with Breckenridge Hills, 63114.

I have placed my order.

In my preteen years on Saturday or Sunday afternoons all the kids would go over to the next village to the Gem Theater. The Gem was up on the Rock Road past Ritenour High School. You could pay a dollar and see three bad movies and were welcome to stay for repeat shows if you wished. The Gem specialized in beach party and Japanese monster movies. A high point of my life was seeing *Godzilla vs. the Thing* two and half times on the same day. All of us were deeply moved when the two miniature geishas, who for some reason lived in what appeared to be a jewelry box, were carted out to sing to the Thing's egg until it hatched.

An enormous disappointment: not being able to go to the Gem on a Friday night when Deborah Walley herself made a personal appearance for the St. Louis area premiere of the film *Beach Blanket Bingo*.

When I was in fourth grade, I hung around the ancient oak tree on the west side of the playground. Decades of students had worn away the earth from limb-sized roots at its base. We would chase each other around its base, careful not to trip but also not to get too far from the trunk. If you weren't touching the tree, you were out. Our favorite topic of discussion was the latest movies at the Gem. I announced the title of the latest bit of vulgarity: a James Bond rip-off movie staring James Coburn. Bobby Reaves—a large white kid with a crew cut—pointed out to me that that could never have happened to me as "they don't allow no niggers in the Gem." My reaction was muted. I was not much of a fighter and he was much bigger than me. He was a dumb guy, too—the kind who has a great deal of trouble with your basic watered-down fourth-grade curriculum. I felt sorry for dumb guys. I knew their lives weren't going to be easy. I remember that, yes, the word stung, but the strongest feeling had been something of a resigned frustration. Already at nine years old I remember how tired I was of having white people assume they knew better than I did the facts of my own life. Which explains maybe why I can with a benign expression on my face and with what may even appear to be patience sit quietly when editors reject my work on the grounds it does not represent an authentic "black" experience. Breckenridge Hills was a good training ground for many aspects of life.

There was an invisible line in Breckenridge Hills and everybody knew where it was. Think of a rectangle. Cut a square out of the middle of the long side of the rectangle. The square is the black part of Breckenridge Hills. Invisible line is perhaps the wrong image. The black part existed almost in another dimension. It was as if you were standing on one side of Baltimore Road—one of the borders of the black part—and you could see clear through to the other side of Breckenridge Road with no interruptions. It was if we were not there at all.

In high school I would be dropped off after some extracurricular activity by the parent of a white friend and many times I would hear the comment, "I never knew these houses were here." I had people deny to my face that I lived in northwest Saint Louis County at all. That black people had lived in that area for more than a hundred years was a moot point.

It didn't hurt that there was only one street that cut through the black part of Breckenridge Hills and that even the roads that ran along its eastern and western borders were not particularly important thoroughfares, traveled mostly by the whites who surrounded us.

Almost all the streets in the black part of Breckenridge Hills were dead ends or cul-de-sacs. Our cul-de-sac was Saint Gabriel Court. We also had Saint Benedict Court and Saint Martin De Porres Lane, all three named after black saints. My parents have lived on Saint Gabriel Court for going on fifty years. With the exception of an apartment they lived in for a few years on Page Avenue in St. Louis, 2 Saint Gabriel Court will have been their only address. Some white people—such as ones who deliver the flowers I send on special occasions—still have difficulty locating them.

It wasn't so much that the black folks of Breckenridge Hills wanted to be invisible or were hiding. Truthfully, with the exception of your generic racist and renegade redneck, things were pretty cool. It's more that no one really cared. Live and let live. No one had had to go to court to buy their houses. The homes had been put up specifically for black families on land owned by blacks. The white folks around us didn't move out when we arrived. Where would they go? Many were much worse off than any of us. It is thought that the working class is the home of racism in this country. Not in Breckenridge Hills. The average university professor I've met is far more prejudiced than the folks who lived around us.

Here is one of the few stories I know that fit into the canon of great moments in the civil rights struggle for African Americans. When my brother was six he wanted to join the Cub Scouts. This was the late fifties. The scoutmaster said no. My father reminded the Scouts that he was a taxpayer and that the pack met in a public school and that he'd hate to have to involve the NAACP. Then the scoutmaster said yes. That was pretty much that. My mother was often the assistant den mother.

Dramatic—slightly—but hardly the stuff of a movie of the week.

Like everyone else, including most of the people who didn't live there, I was repelled by Breckenridge Hills. I knew I was getting out of there from the time I was a small child. I was nurtured in a place where I fit neither in the local community nor in the community at large. I was both specifically and generally wrong for Breckenridge Hills, and everybody seemed to know it. A smart kid in a dumb place. The intellectual among the working class. The outsider from the outside of outside.

What I really believe is, I didn't so much run from Breckenridge Hills as I was pushed away from it. Get him out of here, for God's sakes, before he notices something else.

Both a favor and a curse.

One time, friends from college came to visit. We got in my father's car and took a tour of the area. I showed them all the trashy sights. The Kapriole Room, where bikers had drunken brawls on weekend nights. The American Donuts, where they have the best raised glaze in the world. The headquarters for the local Nazi party. Out front was an acne-scarred guy in full regalia—swastikas and all.

My friends were appalled.

"They let those Nazis have an office here?" they asked.

Of course. Why not? This was Breckenridge Hills in the late seventies. No one paid attention to Nazis. They were just some of the thousands of people I went to high school with. My neighbors ignored them and they went away the way Nazis sometimes do.

So that is it: my chore for the rest of my natural life, I guess. Trying to come to terms with the place where I grew up. The thing is, honestly, I would never live there, or ever live there again if I had to do it all over again. What I feel about Breckenridge Hills is nothing like pain or nostalgia or even any sense of loss. Breckenridge Hills is still very much there where it was.

There have been some changes. Whites have moved into the black part—young families can get a decent house there cheap. Blacks have moved to some of the white parts, as well. There has been some crime, I'm told: a stolen car battery, a busted-in back door. The latest fashion on my parents' cul-de-sac is solid-steel back doors (replacing the previous fads of astro-turf-carpeted porches and aluminum awnings with the family initial painted on).

They love me on Saint Gabriel Court. Not just my parents but all the old folks. I am still like the seven-year-old beauty pageant contestant I had been, except now I wave and smile from the window of my marginally fancy car. They wave back and get on the phone and tell each other that another of the kids has come back for a visit. They are dying one by one, my parents' generation: that does make me sad. Cake plates circulate the neighborhood at the wakes. When my own brother died we had to borrow coolers to keep all the food the neighbors brought us. It's that sort of place. I like that my old parents live in the heart of such warmth.

I could pack it in tomorrow and move back there and be sheltered away in that warmth for the rest of my life and never be heard from again. I think that's one of the reasons I left.

There is a man there who still makes the same circuit he did when we were in high school: up Baltimore and through the playground and down the hill and up Breckenridge Road. A couple of times a day, he does it. It's like his job.

"You know who that is?" my father asked me last summer.

I nodded.

"He's still walking," my father exclaimed. My father is somewhere around ninety. We aren't sure exactly and it doesn't really matter. He's mostly sharp as a tack. Fifty years in his fume-filled auto body garage haven't caught up with him yet. The walker's regularity is some sort of solace for him—that one of the kids is still around and found Breckenridge Hills more than enough for his life, thank you very much. It comforts my father: I really don't get it.

I don't find the story of the walker sad or pathetic or anything, really. I'm just glad it's not me out there circling the block.

Around my ninth birthday I stopped sleeping at night. To this day I keep odd hours. Back then I liked to sleep through the morning and have another nap in the afternoon. Rarely in my life have I seen the sunrise, though during those first sleepless summers of my childhood, the pale blue horizon out my bedroom window was a signal I should close my eyes for a while. I would stay up all night reading and daydreaming. Sometimes I would listen to the "free" radio station that broadcast from the Central West End in St. Louis. They would play records that had been labeled obscene and dare the FCC to yank their license. They would hang a microphone out the window and broadcast whatever or whomever happened to wander by. You could go down there and get on the air if you wanted to. I wanted to. I had many things to get off my chest even then, but I didn't know exactly where the station was and didn't have any way of getting there.

Sometimes at night I would draw pictures. Sometimes I would make up stories in my head.

One night, late, after two in the morning, my room filled with a brilliant white light. I was in my early teens. The light got brighter and it became daylight in the room and I could see where I had strewn my clothes and even the hints of dust in the corner.

"This is interesting," I thought.

I peered around the window frame just like Patty Duke checking out her identical cousin on the old TV show. Outside I could see that our house had been encircled in a ray of white and that even the grass had taken on a color that was new to me.

"Well, this is it," I thought. "They've finally come for me."

I really believed that, too, and I'm not even ashamed to admit it. I believed that it was finally my turn to be abducted by the UFO people. They had the best of intentions. I was excited and only a little scared. I believed they had come and I wanted it to be true. Even after I recognized the beating of the rotors on the county police helicopter, searching through the benign yet deadly silence of Breckenridge Hills for dangerous black folks like me, I still wanted it to be true.

From the Pole Vaulter's Bluff

David Allan Evans

> One of my convictions is that at the center of every poetic imagination is
> a cluster of key images that go back to the poet's childhood . . . poets are
> always revisiting the state of their innocence.
>
> —Stanley Kunitz

When I was about fourteen my older brother, one of the best pole vaulters
in Iowa, taught me to vault, and that quickly became an obsession. I
couldn't get enough of it. My mother used to give up calling me in for
dinner. "Just one more," I'd yell to her, and after that, again and again,
"just one more."

About two decades later, when I published my first book, the first poem
in it had come directly out of the vacant lot next to our house, where we
had our vaulting pit, with crossbars and vaulting poles made out of bamboo.
The poem is called "Pole Vaulter," and its opening lines are

> The approach to the bar
> is everything

Copyright 1995 by David Allan Evans

Unless I have counted my steps
hit my markers

feel up to it
I refuse to follow through

I am committed to beginnings
or to nothing

All poets have one or two poems they consider seminal. This is one of mine. In retrospect, the word *beginnings* in the seventh line may represent the beginning of a new phase of my life. Robert Frost, in his marvelous poem of childhood, says he was a "swinger of birches." If the New England poet was a swinger of birches in his youth, I, a midland poet, was a pole vaulter in mine.

The landscape of my childhood was Sioux City, Iowa, where I was born in 1940. For a midwestern city, Sioux City is a unique mix of urban and rural. (The name itself is an oxymoronic juxtaposition of a Plains Indian tribe's name and a word that evokes Western order and civilization.) Its population has been around 80,000 since I lived there, and yet the city is huge: fifty-two square miles, an area large enough to accommodate the confluence of three rivers, including the Missouri, farms and ranches, packinghouses, and other industry. I feel fortunate to have been raised in both rural and urban settings.

Between the ages of two and eight I lived with my parents, two brothers, and older sister on an acreage. One of my earliest memories is of walking barefoot on cool, hard clods of our freshly plowed potato garden. My father raised chickens and I would sometimes collect eggs from the chicken shed in the morning. On two sides of us were cornfields, on another side, hills, and, a few hundred yards to the east, a deep ravine called Devil's Hollow. On clear nights, because there were no streetlights nearby, the sky was a bowl of stars you could stand inside.

In 1948 we moved from the acreage to a brick house on a railroad bluff on Wall Street. It is mostly this locale, where I lived from the ages of eight to fifteen, that I have revisited obsessively in my memory and my writings:

the brick house (almost forty years later I still remember our telephone number: 88686), and the vacant lot next to it; a ravine at the north end of Wall Street; the railroad tracks, trains, and steam engines, a roundhouse; the Sioux City Soos minor league baseball park across the tracks, and the "pig dump" beyond center field; a steep bluff with creosote steps running down it; a soybean factory on whose roof I was almost electrocuted trying to capture some pigeons; two ponds; the Floyd River, where I learned to swim and where the Ringling Brothers Circus elephants, when the circus came to town every summer, were taken to drink; Woodrow Wilson Junior High and its playground; the Wall Street viaduct; gravel alleys; a deaf and dumb man with an iron-wheeled cart who made a meager living collecting junk; a sewer under Wall Street that my friends and I would walk through with flashlights; a little grocery store owned by a Jewish family named Strongin; a gravel company with its pyramids of gravel; the Jewish Community Center, where I spent a lot of winter nights playing basketball; a steep block of Iowa Street that we used to sled down on Flexible Flyers with waxed runners.

About two miles southeast of our house were the stockyards, Swift's and Armour's packinghouses, Half Moon Lake, and above the lake "Polock Hill," where many Polish packinghouse workers and their families lived. Eight blocks south of us, running parallel to and only a few blocks north of the Missouri, was Sioux City's business district, often referred to pejoratively as "Lower Fourth," a strip of beer joints, restaurants, clothing stores, theaters, and whorehouses (otherwise known as the Virginia Hotel, the Swan Hotel, and the Chicago House, among others). Lower Fourth and the packinghouses were the main reasons Sioux City was known—again, in the pejorative—as "Little Chicago."

This in-town territory—about two miles in circumference, with our Wall Street house in the center—has been the source of at least 70 percent of the images and experiences I've used in one way or another in poems and prose in about three decades of writing. Even the titles of my first two books of poems and book of essays attest to the locale's importance: *Train Windows*, which refers to my habit of watching trains at night from the railroad bluff; *Real and False Alarms*, a fire station at the bottom of Iowa Street, between our house and Lower Fourth; and *Remembering the Soos*, the minor-league ballpark, where I spent many nights with friends.

My teen years were crucial to me; they became a bridge between early and late childhood, between the end of one life and the beginning of another I was gradually discovering.

My main response to the explosion of hormones and the need to prove myself among my male peers was to excel at what I enjoyed most and was good at—sports—and hang out with other athletes, who were among the toughest guys around. I was not one to give schoolwork a lot of attention, and my grades were mediocre. I was a slow reader, and so feeble at math that my teacher labeled me as having a "math block"—this, in front of an entire class. I flunked, and the next semester was sent to Woodshop, the "Opportunity Class," where one day, with other things on my mind than the plane saw I was working with, I nearly cut off a finger.

I do remember my first two coaches at Woodrow, Mr. Speraw and Mr. Barger, and my American History teacher, Mrs. Lefler. She was the one who reminded our class one day that the only "original American" among us was Leroy, who was an Indian from the Winnebago Reservation fifteen miles south. In Sioux City in the fifties, this was not the prevailing opinion on Indians; most considered them thieves and drunks who couldn't hold a decent job or raise a family. Even if I didn't realize it at the time, Mrs. Lefler had given me a gift of a new perspective—not only on my good friend Leroy, but on all Native Americans.

Leroy and his family were not the only minorities in the Woodrow area. The "South Bottoms" near the Floyd River had families of Hispanics, blacks, and even some Asians. I feel lucky to have grown up in a city where I could have nonwhite friends as well as white ones. This racial variety has never been common in small towns in the Midwest.

For me, the hands of Woodrow Wilson's schoolroom clocks could not have moved slower than they did. Whatever the season, I always wanted out—to play baseball or football, swim in the Missouri or Floyd, kill rats in the pig dump, ice-skate, go sledding in the ravine or on the steep streets, mess around down by the roundhouse, or, ignoring my parents' sternest rule, hop a ride on a moving boxcar.

Even though I was not a good student, I had always been able to focus on and even work hard at things I enjoyed. I still have an elaborate pencil design I did at the age of four or five. From an early age I could sit for hours on a sidewalk or at a table, drawing, or making useless gadgets (I called them inventions) out of tin, wood, and cardboard. When I was in the seventh grade a black, jovial doctor named Dobson said I had rheumatic fever (probably a misdiagnosis) and sent me back to school with a note keeping me off the playground and out of sports for the entire spring semester. As my classmates played outside for recess, I drew designs with pen and ink.

The person who had by far the most influence on me in those teen years was my father. He had also been an athlete, and he had the same trait of fixing on something and working hard at it. In his case, the trait may have originated in part from his fairly strict Methodist upbringing, and also from his having to quit school early and get a job to help support his family after the death of his father in a mental institution at the age of thirty-eight. He began to sell newspapers on downtown street corners, and then a few years later he became a pressman's apprentice at the *Sioux City Journal*, where he worked for thirty years, and then, just after I graduated from high school and was starting college, left to become managing editor of his union's magazine in Tennessee. As a college student I had a part-time job in the same pressroom, and those men who had worked with my father spoke highly of his diligence. "He was a worker" was a phrase I heard many times.

But his important work he did at home, pecking away at his Woodstock typewriter in his little corner in the basement, just beyond the clotheslines. This eighth-grade dropout had a powerful ambition to become a writer, and he couldn't get enough of writing, or of the writers he would reread so often that late in his life he would refer to them as close friends: Shakespeare, Montaigne, Voltaire, Anatole France, Herbert Spencer, Thomas Huxley, Tolstoy, Dostoyevski, Charles Darwin, Ernest Dowson, Oscar Wilde, H. L. Mencken, Robert Ingersoll, Marcel Proust, Thomas Wolfe, Robert Benchley, Clarence Day, and many others. Apparently, he had always been a reader. My aunt, his half-sister, once told me there was a feature article in the *Journal*, when my father was around twenty, to the effect that he was determined to read the entire Sioux City public library by the age of thirty. A couple of decades later he would serve on the library board and review books for the *Journal*.

Although he was not an accessible father, since he was so busy with his involuntary and voluntary jobs, he was usually congenial, as well as quiet, even diffident, quick to smile, sometimes moody. And his puritanical upbringing sometimes surfaced. Once when I was around twelve, I told him a joke with the word *turd* in it, and he scorned me and sent me to my bedroom.

He did read to us, occasionally, stories by Ernest Thompson Seton, Oscar Wilde, and Jack London. Seton's *Lobo: The King of the Kumumpa*, about a huge wolf, was my favorite. He read the story many times, and I was the only one of us children who would cry when at the end Lobo was strangled by the lariats of bounty hunters.

My father would read poems or passages from novels or essays to my mother. He had a record of Shakespeare's soliloquies read by John Barrymore, and sometimes he'd bring it out and play it on our old Victrola. I can still recall the piercing, angry voice of Barrymore's *Hamlet* and *Richard III*, and my father, horizontal on his brown Naugahyde recliner, thoroughly absorbed by the poetry. He had an incredible memory for words, better than anybody I've known. His brother, my uncle Elmer, had the same gift, and he could also draw very well. Often when the two of them were together they would drink beer and quote poetry.

I was an outdoor boy at the time and not a reader yet, but I liked listening to the poetry, and to Barrymore's Shakespeare, though I'm sure I didn't understand much of what I was hearing. When you are young, it's easy to be influenced by adults—especially parents—who place such high value on something: in my father's case, the words of great writers.

Yet he never pushed books on his children or anybody. This gentle but intense man simply had books around the house, and showed, by example, how important they can be if you have any inclination to need them. To this day, I cringe whenever I see someone trying to force books or beliefs on others.

Gradually, in my early teens, I began to realize that I not only enjoyed poetry, but, like my father and uncle, I had a talent for remembering it. On my way to the YMCA on Saturday mornings, if I was alone, I would sometimes stop at the public library and go downstairs to what was called the reading room, where there was a record player and a collection of records, some of poets or actors reading poetry. I would put a record on and sit on the couch and listen. This habit was a secret I would share with nobody, least of all my jock friends. In the fifties in Sioux City, sports were for men and poetry was for sissies. That was an absolute.

On that reading room couch the first poem I ever heard *on my own* was Matthew Arnold's "Dover Beach." I didn't understand all of the words, but the rhythms and phrasing enchanted me: I knew nothing about Dover Beach, not even where it was, and yet I felt the lines' dignity and power. I must have wondered to myself how a poet could describe the sea, cliffs, and moonlight with such clarity and force. There was something in the slow, deliberate, serious, drawn-out cadences, in the tone of voice—an actor's named David Allen—that I couldn't have explained to anybody but which I began to love, especially the line containing the "melancholy, long, withdrawing roar," which seemed to go on and on. The emphasis on the word *clash* in the poem's last line—"Where ignorant armies clash by night"—always pleased me. And I could see the images of water in the poem, because I had watched the glittering Missouri from the bluffs at night—the way light "gleams and is gone." I played the poem over and over. It didn't take long to have it by heart, and in my fifties I can still recite it.

One day when I got up the nerve to check out a poetry record and was carrying it home, I was confronted by a high-school kid I knew, a tall, aggressive, outspoken lineman on the varsity football team.

"What's that you got, Evans?" he said.

"Oh, just a record," I said.

"Lemme see it," he said, and grabbed it out of my hands.

He looked at it, and when he saw what it was, he said,

"What's this shit—*pomes?*"

I said "Yeah" sheepishly, took the record back, and went on my way. I heard him behind me, snickering in disgust.

I must have been fourteen or fifteen, standing by one of my father's book-cases, the one in the hallway near the front door. I was picking some books out at random, opening them up, reading here and there. I think I was just curious. I picked out a thick dark-blue book called *The Oxford Book of American Poetry*. Inside the front cover of this book, which I still have, was the price: 35 cents. My father had bought it, along with a lot of other books, at the Salvation Army store down by the viaduct. I started glancing through the pages and came to a poem called "Limited." At Woodrow we were required in English class to read poems, stories, and plays by writers such as Shakespeare, Dickens, Longfellow, Bryant, and Whittier. I had never heard of this author, Carl Sandburg. The word *Omaha* at the end of his poem hit me like a hammer. I was astonished to see such a familiar word in a poem. I hadn't *been* there, but I knew that Omaha was only about ninety miles south of Sioux City. I was also struck by the sounds of the words: for example, the repetition of the same sound in "laughing," "ashes," "ask," and "answers." I knew about trains, of course, living on a railroad bluff. I doubt if I got Sandburg's wry humor at the time, but I must have sensed it: that even if "the man in the smoker" as well as "all the men and women laughing in the diners and sleepers" think they're going to Omaha or whatever earthly destination, they are all, like the rest of us, even the train itself, "hurtling across the prairie" toward oblivion: "scrap and rust." Here, for the first time, was a poet who spoke my language! The words were spare, concrete, accessible, down to earth.

Then I read "Ice Handler." These words were close too. I'd watched the iceman delivering ice to our house, and he was a physical, confident man like the one in the poem.

I also read "Fish Crier." I'd never seen a fish crier, but on the acreage I'd heard the unmistakable sound of wind "blowing over corn stubble in January." At that moment, standing there in the hallway with those poems in my hands, I'd suddenly discovered a few poems that reminded me of things I already knew but were described so convincingly that I would never forget them.

I started writing in my sophomore year in college, first poems and then stories. I had an excellent college creative writing teacher named Howard Levant. A poet himself, he helped me by making specific comments on my poems and encouraged me to read widely and to experiment with various forms of fiction and poetry.

A brief, one-semester Iowa Writers' Workshop experience in the early sixties was a temporary setback for me. Most of the writers in my poetry writing class were from larger, eastern cities and were older and more experienced than I. One afternoon in the student union some workshop poets were giving a reading. A young man named White got up and started reading a poem whose first word was *corn*, and he drew out the word in an exaggerated, loud, derisive way that obviously meant that he didn't like poetry with local perspectives or settings, especially midwestern ones. The audience agreed, clapping and laughing. I felt like the only one not in on the fun.

Some of the workshop sessions were useful to me, and there were some good writers around. But I was intimidated by what I sensed was a strong Eastern bias and didn't think I had much to contribute. Confused, and with my confidence shaken, I dropped out.

I left Iowa City and took a teaching job at a college in Colorado, and slowly, tentatively, trying to forget the Iowa City detour, I began to write poems about experiences and images that were familiar: trains, pigeons, cindered alleys, fistfighting, pole-vaulting, running with a football, working in a packinghouse (another night job while going to college), fishing, and so on. In other words, I began to revisit, through memories, the Sioux City landscapes. Some of these memories were so strong and persistent that the only way I could contain them was to give them some shape in words on paper. The poems I wrote seemed to fall into one of two main categories. One was dynamic and dramatic, such as my poem about pole-vaulting; the other was quiet, static, and introspective, such as my poem about standing where Armour's used to be before it was razed, and which begins,

It is 5 a.m. everything is the same as it was
the moon-hammered faces of the cattle are waiting
the line at the hiring gate is growing minute by minute
you can see the faces of last year or forty years ago.

(I've often wondered whether these two kinds of poems don't reflect a life-style that prefers to alternate bursts of physical energy with long periods of quiet reflection and concentration, in a room alone, writing.) Gradually, I found that I could improve my poems only by revising and rewriting them, which meant, sometimes, hundreds of versions of a single poem or stanza. After I had accumulated a number of poems I was fairly satisfied with, my confidence came back.

I also did a lot of reading. I went back to Sandburg—probably my greatest influence—and I read more recent poets whose sensibilities or backgrounds I could identify with: James Wright, James Hearst, William Stafford, Karl Shapiro, James Dickey, to name five.

And then I had the good fortune to meet James Dickey at a writers' workshop in Boulder, where we talked about a batch of my new poems. I had read some of his poems a few years earlier and remembered at the time feeling a strong kinship. Dickey had also been an athlete, and had an intense interest in evoking the physical life in his poems. He liked my work ethic and reminded me that "Shakespeare never did any pole-vaulting." Those were important words to hear at that point in my writing life, from a poet whose work I admired. The words confirmed what I had been discovering in my own way: it's not so difficult to write like others or to be fashionable. What *is* difficult—and what really matters—is finding a way to consistently say things that couldn't be said by anyone else.

"Poets," says Stanley Kunitz, "are always revisiting the state of their innocence." Kunitz is referring not just to a state of mind but to actual places. For me, if there is one place in my past I need to stay in touch with, it's a railroad bluff in Sioux City, Iowa, a two-story brick house, and the vacant lot next to it with a vaulting pit at the west end. I believe it is possible, in some fundamental way, that my life as a poet began with a flat-out sprint down a dirt runway toward a bamboo crossbar nine feet high.

When Everybody Wore a Hat

Larry Watson

In 1993, Milkweed Editions of Minneapolis published my novel, *Montana 1948*. Set in a small Montana town in the years after World War II, it is the story of the Hayden family and a series of events that threaten to tear apart not only that family but the town itself. Wesley Hayden is the sheriff of Mercer County, just as his father was before him. Wesley's brother Frank is a war hero and the town doctor.

When I completed the novel, something happened that had never happened to me before: the characters and their region would not go away. Ordinarily, finishing a novel, or even a short story, is for me an emptying experience: all those characters, all those settings, scenes, and incidents that I had been holding in my head for years vanish. But with the Hayden family that was not the case. This family would not go away. In an attempt to accommodate their presence, I wrote a "prequel," titled *Justice*, the story of the family immigrating to and settling in Montana.

These two books represented another first for me: I had never written a fiction—of short-story or novel length—in which I stayed so close to my roots, both regional and familial.

Copyright 1995 by Larry Watson

In the wake of the publication of *Montana 1948*, I was often asked, at readings, conferences, and bookstore appearances, about my choice of setting for the novel. It's a good question to ask of a writer, sneakily so in fact. The answer will reveal something not only about the novel's or the poem's content but probably of the writer's character as well. Writers set their work in particular locations for all sorts of reasons they can be consciously aware of and rational about.

In my case, I wanted a frontier feeling, a Wild West undertone to my story that Montana could give it and which my home state, North Dakota, could not. Although the western half of North Dakota can as rightly claim a frontier heritage as any state, it does not send out those signals in the popular imagination as strongly as Montana. Furthermore, state lines are not the only way that boundaries can be drawn. Geography sometimes delineates a region with more meaning and accuracy than do the mapmakers. But I chose that region to write about because, even better than I know the flora and fauna (and one reader has taken me to task for having the wrong kind of tree growing from my fictional soil), I know the people—their values, their tastes, their prejudices, their strengths, their weaknesses, their walk, their talk, their dress . . . When I wrote about Julian Hayden, the family patriarch, I often imagined a photograph of my grandfather seated before his rolltop desk, his sheriff's badge pinned to his vest. When I wanted to describe the heft of a sheriff's badge, I took my father's badge down from my bulletin board and held it in my hand. I know how men of that region hitch their trousers and wipe their boots on the porch step, how both men and women complain about the cold or the lack of rain. Beyond these external details, when I want to flatter myself, I say there is a regional psyche to which I feel I have access.

That access has been aided by the fact that my maternal grandfather was a cowboy in western North Dakota and eastern Montana for many years, before he settled down and filed a homestead claim in North Dakota. My paternal grandfather also homesteaded in North Dakota, and branches of both families settled in each state and visited freely back and forth across state lines.

It's also true that writers choose their settings for unconscious reasons.

The poet James Whitehead says that in poems and stories writers obsessively return to the site of "the first wound." Fair enough. I don't doubt that there are unconscious currents carrying stories to "dock" in Missoula rather than Manhattan. (A strange metaphor to choose for someone who writes of a region so far from an ocean.) But since I am not in therapy and am more interested in accurate, vivid descriptions of place than in self-analysis, I'm going to set aside any deeper implications of why I chose Montana as the setting for my recent fiction.

But amid all those questions about place, I am seldom asked another question about setting, equally relevant, equally revealing. Events happen not only in a place but also in a time, and a writer's choice of a decade, a month, a season, even an hour of the day can be a decision as central to a narrative as a geographical setting. Who we are, individually and collectively, it seems obvious to say, depends as much on when we live as where. Probably more. The Manhattanite of the 1890s has more in common with the Montanan of the same decade than with the New York City dweller of the 1990s. Those decisions about time-setting can also say something about a writer's personality.

For myself, in my recent fiction I've been heading not only West but also into the past. It's been a long time since I set a fiction in contemporary times. And since no one will ask me the question, I'll ask it of myself: Why do I set my fiction in the historical past?

My decision might have to do with nothing more complicated than the fact that there's much I don't understand about the times I live in. Pride in victimization. Casual sex, casual drug use—especially when either practice can be fatal. Families in which children have more power than parents. The eagerness to confess in public what was once deliberately kept private. Politicians who run for office by denigrating their own profession. Artists for whom ugliness and senselessness are worthy aesthetic goals.

I could go on, but the only effect would be to make myself sound more and more like a crank and a curmudgeon. Already I remind myself of the grumpy old man on *Saturday Night Live* played by Dana Carvey, the character who would say something like, "We used to have to eat gruel, nothing but gruel, three times a day, and WE LIKED IT."

Well, I hate gruel. And I hate side pork and lefse and lutefisk and potato soup and beets and some of those other foods that once were dietary staples in the region and time I grew up in. I like microwaves and VCRs and CD players and cars that start as soon as you turn the key. I like them but I don't understand how they work. Just as I don't understand all the behavioral machinery of our times.

I don't want to turn this into a diatribe against our era. My point isn't to judge but simply to say that these phenomena are part of life in the 1990s. It might well be that ten, twenty, fifty years from now these things that I have listed will be seen as trivial, if they are noted at all, of no more importance or lasting consequence than belly-button rings or ESPN2.

Nevertheless, they're here and hard to ignore. For a fiction writer to say "I see all these things around me, but I'm deliberately going to leave them out of my fiction" seems to me an invitation to trouble. For many writers this poses no problem; they're confident enough of their ability to pick and choose, to say, "This I'm going to deal with, this I'm not. This is important, this is not. I can look here; I don't have to look there." I don't have that confidence.

Furthermore, to write about the present seems always to force writers into a critique of their times. I'd rather not do that, leaving the job to the social critics and activists—whose work I often admire.

My solution has been to retreat to the past, in both *Montana 1948* and in *Justice*, to where history and memory have already done some of the writer's work of selecting, winnowing, separating the important from the trivial, the momentary from the universal—back to where the file is closed. (I know, I know. The file is never really closed: history is constantly being reexamined and rewritten. But the picture has stabilized somewhat. Compared to the present, the past is not as shifting, or as shifty.)

So that's an argument for writing about the past, but it doesn't do much to answer the question "*Which* past?" With all those decades, all those centuries from which to choose, why would I choose the first half (roughly) of the twentieth century? More specifically, why do I feel drawn to write about the 1940s and 1950s?

The most obvious reason is that the era is available to me. I was born in

1947, and though I don't believe I have any personal memories of the 1940s that I can trust, many of the family stories that I grew up hearing are of that period. My own first memories—and the first can be the strongest because an emotional aura so often surrounds them—are of the early to mid-1950s, and although we like to give each decade its own name and personality, the years can be as untidy as state borders. What we like to think of as the decade of the sixties is probably more like a span of six or seven years beginning sometime after 1965 and running into the early 1970s. The late 1940s and 1950s were not so dissimilar as decade markers would have us think. That is particularly true of the region in which I grew up.

North Dakota is a progressive state in some respects, but it is slow in others. In technological ways, its 1950s were probably like the 1940s in other regions. Time may pass at the same pace everywhere on the planet, but paved roads, electricity, and indoor plumbing do not come to all communities at the same time.

Television, for example, came later to my hometown than to most of the country, and even when it came later, it came later—programming did not begin until late afternoon or early evening. If we switched on our set earlier in the day, we watched a test pattern or a picture of the state capitol. To some extent then, when I write about the 1940s or 1950s, I am recapturing my childhood. Or trying to. Thomas Wolfe was wrong but Proust was right. We can go home again, but the only paradise is the paradise lost. We can go back to Bismarck, but we can't return to 1956.

In spite of the fact that I might be able to re-create a plains community of the 1940s, the era is not really mine, not in the way that adulthood and maturity are necessary to claim possession. It is my father's time.

During the 1930s and 1940s, my father was a small-town sheriff and, following that duty, served a few terms as his county's state's attorney. My father's professional life was successful, and he moved from one good job to another, usually working as an attorney for a government agency. Nevertheless, I believe it is fair to say that he never had a job that gave him the special satisfaction and reward that he received from being chosen, by the citizens of the county in which he was born and raised, to be their chief law enforcement officer, the man elected to see that wrongdoers were arrested, and, subsequently, charged, brought to trial, and, if possible, convicted. The fact that such jobs possess a measure of cultural cachet did not impress my father, but it did others.

Including me, although I did not know him when he held these jobs in law enforcement. My father was relatively old when I was born, and one of the chief regrets of my life is that before he died I didn't ask him more about what it was like to be a sheriff and a district attorney in that small Dakota town during those years.

I didn't ask enough questions, so perhaps one of the reasons I go back to that era in my fiction is to fill in my father's past and to know the man I couldn't know at that time. Greek myth and Freud tell us that sons symbolically (if not literally) slay their fathers. Perhaps so. But writers have another—and opposite—power: they can create fathers, give them life, albeit of the literary sort.

I began to write about the past when I reached the approximate age that my father was when I was born. I wrote a book about a man who succeeded his father as sheriff of a small town, and although it is fiction I took this much from life: my father followed my grandfather in office. The pattern, of course, has been broken; I'm not sheriff material. But perhaps with my fiction I am doing something to keep the wheel turning.

Writers go back to another time, then, to pay homage to their ancestors, their heritage, hoping to better understand the place, the people, the time from which they came. And thereby to better know themselves.

In his preface to his collected stories, John Cheever wrote that many of the stories came from a time when almost everybody wore a hat. Writing about that same era of hat wearers—the 1940s and 1950s—has offered me the opportunity to explore a theme that preoccupies me: What do men and women do when their heart's yearnings are in conflict with what their society tells them they must do and be?

Couldn't I write about this conflict *and* write about the present? Of course. I have before, and I hope to again someday. Yet I don't think the problem has edges quite as sharp today as it did a few generations ago.

We can probably blame (or thank) the sixties for that. Since that decade, Americans have more freedom. I'll leave it to the sociologists, historians, and moral philosophers—whoever it is who settles these matters—whether this increase in personal freedom is good or bad. I only observe that it is so, and that at least one result seems to be that conflicts between desire and conformity, heart and duty, are not as acute as they once were. As Woody Allen has said, "The heart wants what it wants." Well, certainly it does. And so does the libido. The difference between the present age and an earlier time is, I think, that today the heart more often *gets* what it wants. As I said, I don't know whether that trend, that cultural phenomenon, is good or bad; it is probably, like most things, a combination of both.

I do know that when men wore hats it was far less likely that one of them would publicly take up with the teenage daughter of the woman with whom he lived.

I recently watched Ken Burns's historical documentary on baseball, and one scene in particular struck me. It was footage of the crowd at a game earlier in the century. Now, if you didn't know anything about the game, you would think, from this piece of film, that the spectators in the stands, as well as the players on the field, were required to wear uniforms. There they sat, row upon row of them. All men. All wearing coats and ties. All wearing hats. Not a single shot of a fan with a bared torso painted with his team's colors.

I don't want to be sexist about this. I know there were—and are—more pressures on women than men to dress a certain way, to act a certain way, to think a certain way. Cheever said that his stories are from a period when men *and* women wore hats. He could have added that women wore white gloves and strings of pearls as well.

The "Tranquilized Fifties," Robert Lowell called them, but what were those tranquilizers for? If the era was as becalmed as it is often depicted, why were tranquilizers necessary at all? No, something was churning in those hearts and minds, something that required, again to paraphrase Lowell, Miltown to tame. That turmoil is exactly what I'd like to chronicle in my fiction.

Although I've pulled loose a lot of threads in these pages, I hope I can stitch them tight with this conclusion:

My father always, always, wore a hat.

In the Mountain Ranges and Rain Forests of St. Paul

Patricia Hampl

The sky arced with the strange navy-gold of winter dusk, a color that lasted only briefly, reaching past the leafless elms before real night struck and everything went black (the sky) and white (the world). It was always mid-January, it seems now. Very still, and always frigid, marked with the heroic melancholy of all cold places. Usually it was Switzerland. The Alps, though treacherous, were of course stunning and worth every effort I was making. The twinkling lights of the alpine chalets! The lone campfire of a faithful shepherd tending his shivering flock! The fearful crunch of the snow-crust giving way beneath my icy crampon! But on, on! The pace must not falter—the world lies below in all its thrilling littleness, and I am in the Alps, trudging from peak to noble peak, alone with a majesty unnoticed before this moment, but somehow unaccountably my responsibility from now on.

Much later, when I first heard the music called the blues, music supposedly written out of the South's mossy sadness, the saxophone loneliness of those steely St. Paul winter skies came rushing back as if the blues had been

Copyright 1995 by Patricia Hampl

the missing theme song of those nights, the real music of my childhood, restored finally in the adulthood of a smoky Minneapolis bar.

Sometimes, though, I didn't walk home across the heaped mounds of snow thrown up by the snowplows, snowstorm after snowstorm, on the edges of the boulevards. Sometimes I stayed instead on the frozen sidewalk, ridged with packed-down snow where people hadn't bothered to shovel. Then I was in Russia. The heartless steppes of Siberia. Or risking the wind-swept tundra—whatever, wherever, tundra was. The word *tundra* suggested a degree of physical misery and geographic extremity surpassing the word *steppe*. But steppe was Russian, and carried its own freight of gleaming im-ages: sour-cherry tea in glasses, women in babushkas stirring iron caul-drons, snowdrifts canted into daring curves, as if taunting the commissars of realism with the sleek avant-garde meaninglessness of their forms.

On the ice-packed sidewalk it was not the exalted heights of Switzerland I achieved, but the stripped-bare core of human effort as it inched across the broken flatness of a cold almost sentient in its cruelty. I held my face bravely forward and received the slaps of the wind's ghost-hand. It hurled stinging bits of iced snow right at me. *Take that, and that, and that . . .*

In better weather, I sought out a bench in St. Clair Park, which overlooked the old Czech neighborhood where I was born. I sat still on the middle-class crest of St. Clair Avenue and gazed down on the working-class plain of West Seventh Street as if upon a foreign land. There was even a working man's castle down there—Schmidt Brewery—a nineteenth-century brick industrial fantasia.

The alien field of West Seventh was the past, my family past. And though I felt its immigrant ache, I wasn't looking for "my roots." I was hungry for vista. It didn't occur to me to want out: in true St. Paul hierarchical fashion, I wanted up.

Not simply the up of social advancement. I didn't climb the Alps and brave the Siberian steppes with a burning image of a mansion of my own spurring me forward. When I walked home from school through the real and appalling St. Paul winter, I scaled my imaginary heights not for fun exactly (though it was an utterly absorbing fantasy) but for the important sensation of courage they afforded, and for the golden link they forged with the ordinary.

For the ordinary was where I lived, where we all lived, whether on the showy heights of Summit Avenue or in the laboring lowlands of West Seventh. And those of us stranded in the great intermediate landscape of the middle class—the central artery of St. Clair with all its tidy residential tributaries—were the most ordinary of all. It was the fault of the Midwest, this terrible, empty ordinariness, this vacancy. This was why I had to travel home from St. Luke's grade school via Switzerland and Siberia.

I didn't know yet that all real places are ordinary. I didn't know that a passionate sensation of worthlessness is a mighty engine firing the imagination, and that literature may exist mainly to retrieve the lost and discarded from the trash heap of suspected (or real) disdain. But those walks home in the solemn St. Paul twilight were the beginning of literature for me, the beginning of seeing it before my eyes and in my head, coming from a source I knew not where. Not from books, though I loved books—which is to say I loved other people's imaginations before I encountered my own.

The golden link forged between the imaginary heights of a person's inner, chaotic desire and the larger impersonal fact of a given landscape, a real *place*, forms a bond of enduring attachment. Even fierce attachment. It has nothing to do with mere fantasy, and though it is playful in the extreme, such imagining is deadly serious. I imagined Switzerland, which I had not seen, because I had seen only St. Paul—which I could not imagine. Or to put it another way, I couldn't *believe in* St. Paul: it was too real.

If landscape plays a key role in the formation of the imagination (and certainly it must: it is the primer coat under all we can paint for ourselves and others), then to have absorbed the paradox of love and disdain in one's home place is to be born into an extraordinary imaginative richness. It means you will never be a civic booster, but it also means you will never be able to abandon the haunted avenues of a town where you were convinced *nothing happened*. This, in fact, was what I held against St. Paul, even as a child, peevish and unreasonable as that complaint may sound. How could a place that filled me up with sensation be so vacant, so hidden and removed from the great world and its important and desperate business?

Why I held a city responsible for disappointing my imaginative expectations, I cannot say. But St. Paul was all weather and not much else, I thought, a hollow hierarchic movement from the working class to the middle class. Where was the trouble, where was the romance? Even at ten, walking home from school, I wanted more than landscape: I wanted action. But oddly, I didn't really make up stories as I walked; I made up landscape, using the St. Paul props at hand—delirious winter temperatures and dirty snowbanks scraped into mountains at the side of the street by snowplows. Or maybe the passion firing these constructions of sheer alpine faces and Russian steppes was itself a kind of story making.

And when I went to my father's greenhouse, in the palm house the dozens of old palm trees, ranked on platforms before rental for weddings and funerals, stood like great dusty elephants, waiting for the circus to need them. I entered the palm house, I entered Africa. And in the house where the orchids were kept, of course I traveled down the Amazon where the rain forest kept everything moist as a petal, including me if I stayed for long. How dark the rain forest, how improbable its exotic blooms.

In its quiet and insularity, its deep self-regard and complacency, St. Paul had about it in those years (the 1950s and early 1960s) some of the very qualities people now claim to miss. We lacked drive-by shootings and fretful discussions of children with drugs and guns. We blamed ourselves, mainly, for being provincial. We understood we were the flyover.

When I first read the short stories of Chekhov, and found there the frustrated "provincial capitals" of his Russian interior, I was at home as effortlessly as I had been on the Russian steppes of my old St. Paul. The belief in great places and great deeds, in peak moments and in the depths of the soul, find their most passionate adherents in provincials. For longing is the opposite of possession, and all desire is a supreme act of the imagination. Who but a provincial soul longs for real places as if they were imaginary? And treats the real place as if it did not truly exist?

In this spirit, I wish to tender an apology to St. Paul. Not because I didn't appreciate the particular sweetness of those years, and not because I longed to be elsewhere. It is the Midwesterner's birthright to wish to be elsewhere. We can't help ourselves—we always think the real world is Out There. We make the most resilient New Yorkers because we have it all imagined before we get there: it is the Capital and it always glitters and gleams, holding out its infinite possibility against all the evidence.

Ours was a provincial capital—a contradiction in terms, a place endlessly out of sorts with itself, wanting to sleep, yet crying to be roused. Longing for high drama, but subsiding into Sunday dinner. Wishing to be taken seriously in the halls where decisions are made, but hoping yet more to be patted on the back like a good fellow. Risk is a dog that might bite at any moment; we kept him chained.

My apology, if that is what it is, looks more like recognition than regret. Or maybe it is a form of gratitude. For while I was radiating my sense of worthlessness (and making it a geographic as well as personal deficit), I was actually being absorbed by a radiance slyer and more entire than any I could concoct.

Across the clean provincial slate I was always ready to protest, the four great strokes of the seasons cleaved our lives with dramas of contradictory beauties and miseries. The great river our city had turned its civic back upon coursed below our bluffs anyway, unruly and steady by turns. The little streets with their proud names—Fairmount, Lincoln, Grotto—were all the more intriguing for covering their faces with a bland neutrality.

We were left to our own devices. *What's happening?* we asked each other hopefully when, as teenagers, we met wandering around downtown. *Nothing*, we replied, *nothing's happening.*

But left alone, the details of our lives were isolating themselves, becoming objects that floated free of the environment we refused to acknowledge as our own. Once rejected—once liberated—they were free to establish a deeper allegiance. There, in the splendid residence of the imagination, all the rejected pieces could find their use, their value. They weighed out in lumps of pure gold, all the little rejected coins of our provincial realm.

I will always be grateful for the absences and grudges, the petty prides and needless rivalries of the provincial capital. I cannot see how else a person would learn to imagine—that most essential survival skill—except from the passionate desire to escape the civic harmlessness that only youth understands is a threat to life.

It hardly mattered that the landscape I imagined out of the one I rejected was usually a hopeless cliché ("The twinkling lights of the alpine chalets!" Please. "The lone campfire of a faithful shepherd tending his shivering flock!" Oh, please). What mattered was the passionate reach for the only salvation the mind affords, the lifelong friendship with Imagination that began on the despised streets of my hometown in the solitude of need and the backwater of disappointed vanity.

Most nights now, I walk down Grand for a cappuccino at one of the dozen espresso bars that lately have given us a nightlife and a café society of sorts. Espresso! Drink of the capital, certainly. We seem to be getting there. But under the darkened glass, the orange and fuchsia bromeliads cleave to the slippery bark of the palms, and the rain forest breathes in and out as the Amazon pulls on under the tropical canopy. Still a spindle of smoke rises from the lonely Russian camps on winter nights, still a lone Swiss goatherd lingers faithfully under the streetlights.

The Changing Present

Rosewood

Paul Gruchow

I imagine that every child fantasizes an independent life, freed from the constraints and constrictions of youthfulness and of the household. My own dreams, when I was emerging from childhood into adolescence, centered on some version of living in the wild. I dreamed of being, sometimes in the company of one or another of my cousins, a kind of human coyote, a stealthy and wily opportunist, hiding out by day in groves or cornfields or in the drainage ditches that were such a prominent feature of the landscape I knew, emerging at twilight to hunt or fish or forage for food. I would be, I thought, a nomad, never lingering anywhere so long as to be found out, always living with undetectable lightness upon the land, a hermit, existing at the edges of society but outside of it and unknown to it.

Or I would be a trapper living in a remote northern forest. Because the trapping I knew took place in the late fall and early winter, the world I inhabited in this dream was always wintery. There was a snug log cabin at the center of it. A pair of snowshoes and several pelts on wire stretchers hung on the cabin wall beside the door. Inside, a fire blazed in an open fireplace. A stew bubbled in a cast iron pot above the flames. I would go

---

Copyright 1995 by Paul Gruchow

out in the springtime, my furs loading down my canoe, to a settlement to trade my catch for another year's supplies, and without stopping even for a night, I would turn right around and head back to my snug house in the woods. I dreamed of living where it was wild, but also of living outside of a money economy. I never dreamed of wealth.

My mother, I think, would have preferred a more social life. She loved to talk; she struck up conversations easily with strangers. One day in the Laundromat in town, when the news was of an escapee from the county jail, she discoursed at great length to a stranger on the utter incompetency of the local sheriff. "Why, that man couldn't find his head if it wasn't fastened on," she concluded. The stranger excused himself politely and left the premises. There was a long silence in the Laundromat, punctuated by the slap of buttons against the insides of dryers.

Finally another woman in the place spoke. "Do you know who that was?" she asked my mother.

"Haven't the faintest idea," Mother said.

"That was the sheriff."

Mother laughed loudly. "Well, at least I didn't tell him any lies," she said.

After my father died, she took up ballroom dancing. She grew up in a household kept by Norwegian immigrants with a strong sense of propriety, first cousins bound in what may have been a marriage of convenience. Her parents had adopted my mother from an unmarried Irish girl in St. Louis. My mother married at eighteen. Her husband was a German farm boy, bright but uneducated, a convert as a teenager to a dour Christian fundamentalism of his own making, but worst of all, poor: entirely unacceptable to Norwegian in-laws with social ambitions. My parents had an affectionate marriage, but one in which most forms of public pleasure, especially dancing, were forbidden. By the time my mother was nineteen she had twin babies, her rich and beautiful hair had thinned and turned mousy from the strain of bearing them, and she was living, in the aftermath of World War II, in a twenty-four-foot-square cinder-block basement with a flat ground-level tar-paper roof, and no windows, electricity, or plumbing. So when the opportunity came, in her forties, to dance, she seized upon it extravagantly. For all I know, she even had a drink now and then. One day I drove her home from the hospital. She had undergone a radical mastectomy and was still weak and woozy, but she insisted she'd be just fine. When I called the next day to see how she was doing, she was in high spirits. She had been out dancing until three that morning. "I guess your old mother isn't dead yet!" she said. She had some kind of economic longing, too; for the last year of her life, until her body rejected food, and although there was a day, a neighbor recently told me, when she was down to her last stick of wood for the furnace, she ate a steak for dinner every night.

She laughed a lot, especially at her own jokes, always a bit too boisterously. I do the same, and so did my grandmother on my father's side. My grandmother laughed with pleasure, but she also laughed whenever anything went wrong. The more dire the news, the harder she laughed, not that she thought travesty funny, but because she had a heavy sense of fate. When things went wrong, what else could you do? You could never tell, when my grandmother laughed, whether she was amused or unbearably sad. I am the same way. When I laugh, I hear the loud, ambiguous laughter of my mother and grandmother.

My father would have liked, I think, a life of greater adventure. He was the youngest of the five children in his family who lived past infancy, and the only male. His ancestors were Polish farmers, early followers of the Reformation who fled oppression in their own country, first settling around Berlin, and then immigrating to the United States. My grandparents grew up in the rich farming country of northwest Iowa, too late to homestead; my father, because of an inheritance of my mother's, was the first Gruchow in his direct line to own land. Grandfather, as was the peasant custom, dutifully served his own father until his twenty-first birthday; on that day, he got married in morning to a German girl who did laundry for the wealthy folks who summered in the Iowa Great Lakes. On the afternoon of their wedding day, grandfather put up a load of hay while grandmother went off to do a load of wash. Perhaps they were shivareed that evening by friends and neighbors, but a honeymoon was out of the question. Eventually they migrated from Iowa to much poorer land in Minnesota, where they lived out their days as farmers on shares. In retirement, grandfather kept a few chickens and watched television; grandmother rubbered on the party telephone line, kept track of the comings and goings of the neighbors, and read children's books, the only kind she could read. They were, I would say, happy; at least they never wanted or expected any other kind of life. Three of their children stayed in the neighborhood; they were generous but stern grandparents; we grandchildren feared Grandpa's razor strap, with which we were spanked—the shame of it being worse than the sting.

Although my father was a gifted student, he left school after the eighth grade to go to work. Like his father, he worked at home without pay until he was twenty-one, when he married my mother, whom he had met at a roller-skating rink. The couple settled in the neighborhood where they had been raised. There they remained for the rest of their lives, venturing beyond it, so far as I can recall, except for an occasional Sunday afternoon picnic, only five or six times: a honeymoon trip to the Black Hills, a trip one winter to New Orleans, one to northern Minnesota to go blueberrying, one or two trips to the state fair in St. Paul, and one to Minneapolis to attend my own wedding. My father owned two suits in his lifetime—the dapper doubled-breasted navy one he was married in and the gray polyester one he was buried in—and four cars—a Model A Ford, a Chevrolet, and two Studebakers. The last of the Studebakers, a pink Lark, stout and gaudy, was, I believe, the single material indulgence of his life. He gave something close to half of the family income, after farm expenses, to the church. He had a keen awareness of the many people in the world who were less fortunate than he. This was not a decision about which the rest of the family was consulted, nor one in which they would likely have concurred.

My father's dreams were centered on lost worlds. He was a romantic, not in the perverted sense in which the word is now customarily used—fanciful, impractical, unrealistic—but in the older sense: he was an idealist, attracted to the idea—so far from his own life—of adventure, a celebrant of nature, of the ordinary person, of freedom of spirit. It seems to have been forgotten that to use the label "romantic" to dismiss any idea currently out of fashion is to condemn it for its devotion to principle rather than expediency, to ordinary human beings rather than to those who would exploit them, and to freedom from intellectual tyranny. I, like my father, am, in the old sense, romantic; I do not believe that idealism is a delusion.

The lost world of Atlantis fascinated my father. In this, I suppose, he was under the influence of Ignatius Donnelly, Minnesota's great agrarian rabble-rouser and sometimes crackpot scholar. So did the story of the Arcadians; his was the romance of pastoral peacefulness and simplicity. One still meets people like him in the countryside, people who have been to the city only once and thought that was one time too many, who feel awkward even in the big rural county-seat towns, who abhor crowds, bustle, and fanciness, who might enjoy racing stock cars at county speedways on the weekends but are discombobulated by the aggressive swirl of traffic on urban free-for-all-ways, people perfectly content to be who they are and where they are. One also meets the same kind of person in cities, sometimes in high places, the sort of person who went to the countryside once for a weekend and thought to die of boredom, who shudders to imagine the cloying, stultifying, shabby meanness of life in the kind of hamlet where the only restaurant serves beef commercials and there isn't a good show or nightclub or store that sells a shirt not made in Taiwan within a hundred miles. The only difference between the two, really, is that one kind of person is thought to be a bumpkin, a hayseed, a hick, and the other is regarded as a sophisticate. What divides them, mainly, is not who they are but what they have.

My father was also inspired by the Cajuns, by the story of their lonely wanderings in search of a place to live in peace, until at last they came to the bayous of Louisiana, a swampy land, teeming with snakes and alligators and mosquitoes, that nobody else wanted, and of how they made there a vibrant culture suitable to the place. Our solitary family trip out of state, to Louisiana, was, I now understand, a kind of pilgrimage. It is fashionable at the moment to reread the settlement history of the continent as a morality tale: the venal avarice of the conquering horde. One such account that I happen to have on my desk describes "the European predilection to kill first and ask questions later." I doubt that this characterizes the average settler, who was, I think, an Old World failure in search not of a new world to conquer but of a refuge, a place with a few cows, a garden, a house of one's own, as far away from trouble as possible. It is the worst kind of sentimentality to suppose that bad results generally flow from bad intentions. Often, our best intentions are the ones that confound us.

The refuge my father dreamed of was in Alaska, where it was still possible to homestead. *Alaska* magazine was the only one he ever subscribed to. My father often displayed, as if it were an icon, a photograph, gleaned from the magazine, of some huge cabbages growing in the Sitka valley. He held them in the kind of regard that an art connoisseur might have for a rare oil by an Old Master. The place was, to him, never merely Alaska, but the Land of the Midnight Sun, where a person could live free and unencumbered, simply, off the land. As a practical matter, living off the land required a natural system still more or less intact. My father did not want to conquer the land, to build an empire, or to leave any legacy other than his example. He mocked the back-to-the-land hippies of my own generation, but not because he had any fundamental disagreement with their dreams; it was their ineptness that bothered him. He was a dreamer too, but a dreamer who could build a house, fashion a tool out of scrap metal, prune an apple tree, shear a sheep, and hive a swarm of honeybees.

I was, I think, ten the afternoon I decided to act out my own dream. Mother was at a ladies' aid meeting; I had only recently been released from the humiliation of having to accompany her. Dad was in the field. I gathered the quilt and pillow from my bed, stole a quart of dill pickles from the cellar, cut a cabbage and pulled some carrots from the garden and piled these onto the quilt, added a box of matches, an empty tin can, a length of fishing line and a hook and bobber, gathered the ends of the blanket up into a bundle, and set off down the field road toward the slough.

The road, about a third of a mile long, skirted the plum thicket on the edge of the farmstead grove and then turned north along the property line toward the cattail marsh. The plums were still green, but there were a few ripe wild grapes, tart, mostly seeds and skin, as refreshing as lemonade. I picked a bunch, tucked them into my bundle, and trudged on down the lane, two narrow dirt tracks with a growth of weeds—plaintain, foxtail, pigeon grass—between. On both sides of the track rose rows of corn tall enough to hide a man, their ears just at the milk stage. I plucked foxtail stems as I walked and chewed on their sweet, succulent ends.

The field was level, good black prairie loam soil, all the way to the slight ridge that, even in winter, hid the marsh from view. Over the ridge, the land made a shallow basin, longer than wide, running northeast to southwest and draining at its southwestern end, when the water was high, into a tile; the slightly lower basin on the neighbor's land had already been drained. Ours hadn't, I think, because Ed Will was too old to be interested in new capital investments.

The slough was oval; its shape was accentuated by the concentric rings of vegetation that defined it: row crops on the uplands; then a gray-green ring dominated by the weedier prairie plants: common milkweeds, goldenrods, sunflowers, prairie dock; in the dampest soils and shallowest waters, a few swamp milkweeds, cup plants, joe-pye weeds; then the thickets of cattails and hidden among them the houses and hidden waterways of muskrats; and then the gray-blue, irregular oval of open water at the center of the marsh, which lasted into August only in the wet years; in the dry ones, the water evaporated away, the water plants shriveled up, and a lacy network of deep cracks, like the surface of an old china plate, opened in the marsh bottom, which had an ashen glaze of alkaline precipitates. In the driest years, one could go walking on the marsh bottom, stepping over its dark cracks, the shells of pond snails and the brown tubers of cattails crunching underfoot, a sound as arid as the landscape itself.

At the upper end of the pond, there was a woodpile, the remains of a big old cottonwood tree that had once grown there, in which I had trapped both a weasel and a skunk. Perhaps now in the August heat it sheltered a snake. I would have to go there later to investigate. But for the moment I was content to spread my quilt beneath the other cottonwood tree, the one still standing at the lower end of the pond, just beyond a small thicket of willows. I loved it for its ragged heights. As I lay there gazing up into the sky, it sometimes looked as if the tree would snag one of the cottonball clouds of prairie summer, so that I might, at last, climb up and get the feel of a cloud. I loved the cottonwood for its thickly textured bark, as brown and furrowed as my grandfather's hands. I loved it for its heart-shaped leaves, clattering in the breeze on their petioles, making a sound like gentle summer rain. I loved it for its shade, the thin, dappled shade of a solitary tree, which admitted the sun in yellow patches, as through the panes of a window into an empty room on a quiet afternoon. It was the light and shade of close summer afternoons, slightly moist, warm as a blanket, lazy, accompanied in the background by the *okaleeing* of blackbirds and the musty smell of marsh water and the feel of damp earth between bare toes.

There was nothing better to do on such an afternoon in the shade of such a tree than nothing: the elicit sweetness of idleness when there was, as always, work that needed doing, work that would have to wait. Nothing but to wait and watch, to listen, to doze, to dream, to pluck apart the petals of a flower, to spy on leafhoppers and spittlebugs, to host a tree frog in the palm of a hand, to imitate the droning of a bumblebee, to anticipate the fall of a green leaf. Donald Hall reports, in *Life Work*, the meaning of happiness, as it was reported to him by an Indian acquaintance: *absorbedness*. I know, as much from boyhood afternoons at the marsh as from anything, what he meant: those brief moments in life when one is so occupied as to forget time, when time has become a translucent pair of wings.

I prided myself on my ability to tell the time by the sun. When I saw that it was after five o'clock, I made a meal: a wedge of the cabbage, a couple of the carrots, several dill pickles. I intended to forage for food and to try my hand at cookery, but these were efforts that might be made later, when I had settled in. The garden food, in any case, ought to be eaten while it was still fresh. I would have liked a glass of Kool-Aid, I had to admit. It was a good and satisfying meal; if only I had thought to bring a tomato, too. Our garden flourished in an old pasture in soil rich with the residue of animals. We gardened organically, and many of the seeds we planted were, we would say now, heirlooms, saved from the best plants of previous seasons, the ones prized for their vigor and for the intense flavor of their fruits. They were the end product of generations of discriminating selection. The sort of gardener I knew when I was growing up was a small-time plant breeder and, although the cooking was generally plain, an epicure: someone who judged a vegetable more by its taste than by its appearance. Our everyday kitchens were supplied, as I was for my purloined repast, with ingredients so fine that money could not buy them. It was one of the ways in which we were, although impecunious, rich.

After the meal, I climbed into the cottonwood tree, took a lofty seat with a view of the marsh, and settled in for the evening show. It was a show without much of a plot, although I never tired of it. The shadows lengthened; the light assumed a late, golden radiance; mama ducks took a turn around the pond with their cheeping chicks in tow; muskrats swam here and there, submerged except for the upper third of their heads, making brown arrows in the water from which their wakes spread like feathery tails; the evening showed its colors; twilight rose, as if out of the water, and spread like fog; the birds fell silent; the first stars came out; the crickets began to fiddle; and then there was the moon, and the moon's soft blue light, floating upon the darkness of the submerged earth, or held aloft upon the shimmering ostinato of the crickets, a sound that accentuated the silence.

I began to feel sorry for myself as the night and the silence deepened. Nobody had come looking for me. Did this mean that I was not missed? Had no effort been made to find me? Perhaps days would pass before anybody noticed that I was not present. There would be some chore and nobody to do it, I supposed, and then somebody would finally look around and say, "You know, I haven't seen Paul lately, have you?"

"Now that you mention it, I don't think so."

"He always was one to disappear when there was work to do."

I, in the meantime, would be dead, drowned in the muck of the pond, or struck by lightning in a passing thunderstorm, already bloated and starting to smell. There would be flies crawling in the sockets where my eyes had been. When they found me in that condition, they'd be sorry. Then there'd be a few tears for poor old Paul.

I was a little teary myself as I climbed down from the tree and wrapped myself in the quilt. My mother had made it of old flannel shirts and pajamas and worn-out overalls. There were twenty years of family history in that patchwork blanket, which had been mine for as long as I could remember. It felt good to be embraced in it now and to lay my head on a familiar pillow. I removed my eyeglasses and put them in the tin can for safekeeping.

The bright drawbridge of the Milky Way dissolved into a vague glow. In a distant farmyard a dog barked.

I awoke in the dark hour just before dawn when the rabbits have come out to feed in the dewy grass, and the owls are settling into their daytime roosts, and the songbirds have stirred and one at a time begun to sing, the hour of the day, in one strand of Native American mythology, when all creatures sing to encourage the plants to drink the dew.

Nothing compelled me to rise from my bed beneath the cottonwood tree, and for a long time I didn't. This was the first of hundreds of mornings that I have spent in out-of-the-way places listening and watching as the dawn opens the day. When I arise in my house, brew a pot of coffee, read the morning newspapers, and go to my study to begin the day's work, I have submitted myself, usually pleasantly and productively, to the discipline of the clock. But there are other ways to follow time. One alternative is not to live hour by hour but moment by moment, understanding that a moment might last indeterminately, to live, that is, from experience to experience, as I do, perhaps instinctively, when I travel into nature. Dawn is one of the moments of this kind of time.

One of my sisters believed when she was a child that salt cooled hot food. This exasperated my father. "If salt cools food," he would say, "then tell me why it melts ice."

"If salt melts ice, why isn't it hot?" she would reply.

They had the argument a hundred times, both of them absolutely certain of their reasoning.

One afternoon, on our way home from a visit to our grandparents, Dad struck a pheasant with the car and killed it. He stopped, collected it from the road ditch, and that night we had it for supper. It was delicious, if a meager meal for four, but my sister absolutely would not eat her portion.

"It's *dead*," she said. "I'm not going to eat any dead pheasant."

"But dear," Mother said, "you eat chicken, and chicken is dead too."

"No it isn't. Anyway, I'm not going to eat any dead old pheasant."

"Would you prefer to have your pheasant served live?" Dad asked.

But there was no use in pushing her. My sister wasn't going to eat that pheasant, and she knew how to throw up at will if you tried to make her eat something she didn't want. It was a skill I vastly envied.

I suppose there are people who never make the visceral connection between death and meat on the table.

I believed in the All-Seeing Eye of God. I believed that it was an actual eyeball, floating around in a triangle, just like the picture in *Luther's Small Catechism*. For a time, no argument could have persuaded me that there was not always, in the sky just beyond my own sight, an enormous eyeball in a gigantic triangle, keeping watch over me.

My grandmother knew that the garden had to be planted by the moon.

My grandfather could douse for water with a willow stick.

My mother was certain that when your nose itched, someone was talking about you.

My father believed that Central Standard Time was God's time and that the legislators who tampered with it to make Daylight Savings Time were engaged in a blasphemy.

At the marsh, I realized in an intellectual way for the first time that there were many possible ways to measure time, that hours and minutes constituted an idea, an attitude toward time, and were not inherently attributes of it. The possibility occurred to me then that there were other things I devoutly believed to be facts that weren't facts at all. I tried to think of something that was certainly a fact, something not based upon an assumption or a way of seeing, and realized that I did not know what it might be. I came then to the conviction, which I still hold, that what one believes is more powerful than what one knows, and that there is no escaping belief, the shorthand every human being must resort to in the face of the impossibility of knowing everything. Whether it is possible to know *anything* in any final sense remained, I decided, to be seen.

I had more practical considerations on my mind when I finally did get up. I needed to think about some kind of shelter. What would I do when it rained? When winter came? I walked around to the other end of the marsh to inspect the wood pile. Perhaps its pieces might be rearranged into some kind of hut. But that, I soon saw, was unlikely. I thought of a dugout such as the first white settlers in this country made, but the slopes in the vicinity of the marsh were gentle, the digging that would be required formidable, there was no prairie turf left with which to sod it, and I had neither a shovel nor the materials for making one. I could raise a tepee, but where would I find the skins, and how would I tan and sew them? The most logical solution, I thought, was to make a wigwam. The willows might be cut and bent to shape, and there were plenty of cattails, from which mats for thatching might be fashioned. I cut an armful of cattail leaves, hauled them to my shelter beneath the cottonwood, and set to work. But the leaves were not as pliable as one would have thought; they had a tendency to crease when they were bent too far; and when I had assembled a whole mat it was not clear to me how to bind it; in any case, it hardly looked waterproof; either there was a better way to do the weaving or one would need to make a daunting number of mats and layer them. I wasn't prepared for these technical difficulties. Fortunately, rain did not seem imminent, and winter was months away.

In the books I particularly admired at this stage of my life—*Robinson Crusoe, The Swiss Family Robinson, Huckleberry Finn*—these difficulties never seemed to emerge. The people who got shipwrecked on islands or floated away down rivers, apparently, were naturally handy; the right tool always just happened to be in the chest that had washed ashore; and the places where they landed were amazingly rich in just the resources one needed to survive. My own thoughts, over a lunch of the remaining garden vegetables and the last of the pickles, turned not upon resourcefulness but upon thievery. I would have to sneak back to the farmyard in the night and help myself to a few supplies. If Crusoe could ransack ships, why couldn't I have a go at the toolshed? I'd return the stuff, of course, when I had finished with it.

After lunch I took a nap. I was a free boy now, and such luxuries were available to me. Then I needed to think about supper. My life as a hunter and gatherer had begun. My first thought was to catch a fish. I didn't much like fish but it was the only game I was prepared to catch. I whittled a digging stick and poked around in the soft furrows of the cornfield until I exposed a couple of earthworms, baited my hook, and tossed it out into a muskrat channel. Later, I could see, I was going to have to make a raft. It was a quiet, warm afternoon and nothing much was stirring, but it was pleasant to sit there imagining the huge bullhead that was about to strike. There weren't any bullheads in the marsh, as I might have known if I had thought about it. I would have done better to have gone after a mess of crayfish, which abounded there, but I didn't yet know how delicious they are, and I had a profound fear of things that snapped. Once when I was much younger I found a flashlight bulb in a dresser drawer I had been told to stay out of and managed to swallow it. The next time I rummaged, despite being sharply forbidden to do so, in that drawer, I got my fingers caught in the mousetrap that had been set there to teach me a lesson. Not only didn't I forget it, but it was years before I dared to get close again to anything that snapped. My grandmother had a case with a spring-loaded lid in which she kept her eyeglasses. I was afraid even to approach it.

Eventually I despaired of catching a fish for my evening meal. What else might I find? Some corn. I went up into the field and picked a couple of ears. And frog legs! Why hadn't I thought of them before? They were, I had heard, a delicacy. If there is one thing a country boy knows how to do, it is how to catch frogs. In short order, I had pounced upon two big leopard frogs and slaughtered them. After that, I was at a loss. Should one cook the whole carcass? Just the legs? Should they be skinned? How should they be cooked? The possibilities were mercifully limited. I severed the legs, found it difficult to get a grip on anything so small and slick, and so concluded that they must be cooked unskinned, boiled, obviously, since the only utensil I had was the tin can. I would have to think later how to pilfer a skillet. I made a fire, brought a bit of water to boil in the can, and dropped in the legs. While they cooked, I ate the corn raw. It was surprisingly good, I thought, even without salt and butter. Then I considered the legs, which had shriveled to almost nothing and turned an awful color of gray. I poked at one of them with my knife, extracted a bit of flesh, swallowed it without tasting, and gagged anyway. Perhaps I didn't want to eat dead frog legs after all.

This depressed me deeply. I could not have said what I was depressed about, but it was the realization that my escape into the wilderness of the slough was not practical, that the place was, rich as it seemed, too narrow in its resources to sustain me, and that I was unequipped to take advantage of even such resources as it did offer. I had dreamed of a retreat into a world long past, but it was the present world, I saw, in which I would have to make my way.

I sat beneath the cottonwood tree as the dusk rose again from the earth and spread like smoke. I cut a length of green willow branch, as my grandfather had shown me how to do, worked its bark loose and slipped it off, carved an airway and a series of sound chambers in the naked stem, made finger holes in the bark, slipped it back onto the stem. With my crude flute I joined the blackbirds in a song to welcome the night.

Later, in the light of the moon, I gathered my things into the folds of the quilt, slung the bundle over my shoulder, and made my melancholy way back to the house. I felt sheepish when I arrived at the breakfast table the next morning and was relieved to be welcomed as if I had never been away. My parents, I realized, knew where I had been all along. I had been out hunting for the way home.

How I Became a Broken-In Writer

Linda Hasselstrom

I used to think that men could stand more punishment than women, but
I was wrong. In winter a girl wears a fox skin, but her brisket is bared to
the weather, and there ain't nothing on her that's warmer than a straw
hat, but she don't pound her feet nor swing her arms. If she's cold
nobody knows it. If a man would go out dressed this way, there ain't
doctors enough in the world to save him. No sir, a woman can go farther
with a lipstick than a man can with a Winchester and a side of bacon.

—Charles M. Russell, *More Rawhides*, 1925

I always wanted to be somebody, but I should have been more specific.

—Lily Tomlin

At nine years old, I was baptized into ranch life on the arid western South
Dakota prairie and bought my first horse, a fat old sorrel mare, for eighty
dollars. I'd read *Black Beauty* books for four years, dreaming of a lean cowboy in a white hat riding beside my tall black stallion across a fantastically
green plain.

At forty-seven, I happily rode the grasslands of the same ranch on an

Copyright 1995 by Linda Hasselstrom

elderly gray gelding beside my second husband. I'd never married a cowboy, and didn't know anyone who owned a white hat. By the time I turned fifty, my life was utterly changed.

I learned about hard work when I was so young I still thought it was fun. Riding was pure pleasure; on horseback beside my father's Tennessee walker, with fencing pliers and staples jingling in our saddlebags, I learned to evaluate the condition of water holes and cattle. Years of being close to cows in various moods taught me respect for their instincts and intelligence; I could tell the old whiteface whose tits got sore when she calved from the one who licked my ear when I milked her. Sometimes, eyeball to nostril with a furious bovine, I understood by his facial expression which way to jump. I learned to like cattle, to love sun's heat on my back and strong arms. I discovered ecstasy in riding the prairie and fixing fences alone; seasoned by labor, I prized the days my father trusted me to follow his commands alone.

Learning to climb on my bareback horse from a rock in the pasture enlightened me: my mother's work—cooking and cleaning, mending and gardening—was not nearly as fascinating or dangerous as my father's. Free from supervision, I rode my horse over the skyline at every opportunity; I carried a notebook to record what I saw, and questioned old-timers and books. I started a novel featuring myself as an Indian maiden riding an untamed stallion. Learning poise and confidence in my horsemanship, I spent less time cleaning my room. Mother told me to wear a hat to protect the fragile skin I inherited from her; otherwise, she said, "you'll look like an old boot by the time you're thirty." The broad-brimmed hat blew off, unless I tied it under my chin with strings that choked me; usually I wore a cap.

My mother, whose marriage to my stepfather brought me to the ranch, is a bird-boned blue-eyed belle who makes me feel huge and awkward; my boyfriends invariably whispered, "Your mother's beautiful!" Courageously, she left her own ranch childhood for secretarial training in a big city; after two divorces, she found her way back to her own country to raise her daughter. After she married my stepfather, she must have missed city life, but dedicated herself to homemaking and beguiling me into domesticity. Enrolled in 4-H, I was irritated at having to learn to sew and cook; forty years ago, girls couldn't enroll for a horse project.

When I was fourteen, my father retired his old team of workhorses and bought a new John Deere tractor he said was my birthday present. Thereafter I spent long hot days in the hay field, mowing and raking. I knew it was work, and I was proud of doing it, but I also enjoyed watching buzzards and studying coyotes. Did people in speeding cars on the highway know I was sweating on my tractor to provide them with beef? When I overheard my father say to a neighbor, "She can mow as much hay as a man," I was proud; I tucked doubts behind a locked portal in my brain.

My mother and grandmother declared it improper for girls to work with cattle; a lady learned domestic skills to follow tradition: attending college long enough to marry, then having children. My father's culture decreed that wives and daughters who worked outside only proved their men couldn't afford hired help, or adequately support them. The dilemma tangled his thinking. A hired man would have to live and eat meals in the house with his daughter, or in a bunkhouse we didn't have, and couldn't afford. My mother refused to add extra work to her load, so he chose the lesser of two evils. He put his growing daughter to work, reminding me I'd go to college after high school. Even fresh from the city, I rode like I'd been born on a horse; I loved ranch work despite the rules my father added every time he thought of a new danger, or saw unladylike behavior. For years he shoved the calves up the chute himself, so I wouldn't get kicked, and ordered me out of the corral while he castrated, even if the two of us were branding a hundred calves. Helping brand at neighboring ranches as a teenager, still considered a newcomer, I drew the lowest jobs. I wrestled calves in ankle-deep mud, and held a leg while a man castrated. Once I'd seen every detail, I refused to leave at my father's command; he glared and sliced off the end of a calf's testicle without another word. I was nearly forty before I castrated a calf; when father directed my husband, George, to do it, I had to show him how.

Growing older, I grew stronger, while hired men cost more and knew less. One man we hired drank up his whole week's wages on payday, then drove through two of our wire fences trying to get home. Father stopped hiring outsiders and paid me in cash and cows. I registered my own brand and tucked money into a college savings account; I bought second-hand clothes.

When I talked about coming back to the ranch after college, my father shrugged. Once in a while, I tripped shoving a cow through a gate and got kicked in the knee. "Don't think about it and it won't hurt," my father said. After a day in the dusty corral sorting cattle, I got headaches so severe I cried; if mother heard me, she gave me an aspirin. "Think of something else," she'd say. "Go to sleep."

As college loomed, mother encouraged my dating the sons of business-men in town, trying to keep me away from local boys so I wouldn't marry a rancher. I scribbled in notebooks and wrote poems; after studying jour-nalism in high school, I worked one summer for the local city daily. During my first graduate year, I worked on the night staff of a city newspaper and made a hundred-twenty-mile round-trip daily to college classes. The editor wouldn't let me leave the office to chase stories; "Too dangerous for a woman," he said. Fired with journalistic zeal and the energy common to twenty-three, I considered going to Vietnam as a war correspondent. Muddled by alternatives, I married another newspaper reporter instead.

Once a Baptist minister, Daniel was thirty—seven years my senior—and divorced with three children; he sang in bars on his nights off. During our traditional wedding ceremony in the little white church in my hometown, my skull reverberated with dreams of two or maybe four red-haired chil-dren, riding the prairie behind us. We moved to Missouri, where Daniel signed up for graduate work in philosophy; I taught journalism at a wom-en's college while completing an M.A. in American Literature for "some-thing to fall back on," as my wise and cynical mother advised. During the seven years of our union, my outgoing husband transformed himself first into a bearded, pipe-smoking philosophy professor, then a jazz singer, then a writer. I wrote daily in my journals, but I worked two jobs and seldom finished a poem. Competing with more energetic women for my husband's services frustrated me until I left him. When I came back that fall, he and his band were living in a rundown house, eating rice and kidneys, the only meat they could afford. Even ranchers seldom eat kidneys, but plains-raised women recognize need; I cleaned the house and started feeding the band with another teaching job.

Still searching for fulfillment, my husband took his velvet-voiced younger brother to Europe; while they made a fortune singing in military nightclubs, he told me, they'd stay with a third brother stationed in Germany. Disenchanted, they headed home and got to St. Louis before running out of money. As I drove to collect them, my reliable van burst into flames—another omen I missed. Reconciled, we moved back to the ranch in a last attempt to put our marriage together. When he was too broke to pay his support payments, I taught at a college seventy miles away. During the first semester, I learned of new girlfriends and divorced him the summer I turned thirty.

By contemporary standards, I realized with relief, my chances for marriage were expired; only a few of my poems had been published in the twelve years since I had finished high school. Skedaddling back to the ranch, I pitched hay for my father in daylight and wrote whenever I had a moment alone, wondering if I could tuck a teaching job into my spare time; I barely survived on the salary my father paid.

Neighbors teased me for wasting time on education since I'd ended up returning to the ranch and applauded me for my part-time teaching jobs; when I turned down full-time teaching, they were puzzled. But I'd discovered a *need* to write, and could arrange ranch work around it. Coming back to the ranch altered my perspective on myself, and on the problems that concerned my neighbors in a different sense than they worried my friends in the city. I found material everywhere. Reading western history, I talked with my neighbors about their lives. I studied and observed the environment of our land—and conflicts between the new ecological awareness and my ranching life-style. Behind my learning stood my father's deep knowledge of our ranch.

Then my parents started going to Texas in the winter, leaving me alone to take care of the cattle. I fit my writing around cattle-feeding chores in the winter, spring calving, and summer haying. Slowly, my father began to understand that I could lift more than he could; my mother conceded that writing must be important to me, since I had stuck with it so long, but she wished I would clean house more often.

The naked facts of my second marriage sound like the plot of a soap opera. After my first husband moved out, I finished my teaching contract.

Two men among my students that spring became part of each other's lives, and mine. George and Jerry discovered muzzle-loading rifles and modern rendezvous together; George once dragged Jerry from a burning tipi. Twenty years later, Jerry came to us as soon as he knew George was dying, and sat by his bedside with George's mother and me. George died in 1988; when I left the ranch five years later, I moved in with Jerry.

George was an air force veteran, retired on disability when Hodgkin's disease—cancer of the lymph system—nearly killed him the first time. When I met him, he'd recovered twice from near-fatal bouts and was freshly divorced, with a young son, Michael, to support. For five years, we waltzed around each other, breaking up and reuniting before we finally married in early 1979. George insisted he married me only to save my reputation: the neighbors had seen his blue van parked in my driveway for a week after a blizzard.

He accepted both my need to write and my compulsion to stay on the ranch. He was determined to learn to be a rancher, and he listened patiently to my father's orders. If my father gave us a job George knew he could do alone, he sent me home to write. For nearly ten years, we worked with my father, as I grew more deeply committed to writing.

About that time, I began to truly see the strong women around me; imitating my father, I'd grown up sneering at women's work. Now I began to consider the choices these women had made. Some, like my mother, shaped their lives to fit men's desires for so long they knew nothing else. Others appeared to conform, but created considerable freedom within those constraints.

When I moved back to the ranch after my divorce, my closest neighbor was a young woman who had been in grade school when I was in high school; in a few years Margaret was my closest friend. She and her husband kept bees and ran cattle a mile from our ranch. Soon we began attending meetings of an environmental group together, trying to find practical ways to conserve resources in our daily lives. During long public meetings, we scribbled notes to each other, and on the drive home we cheerfully disagreed about religion and politics. Whenever I dropped in for tea to show her an article I'd found on an environmental topic, she had several clippings about women or ranching to show me.

I knew Margaret was a real ranch woman, but I was still surprised at her courage when her back was broken in an automobile accident one Thanksgiving Day. She remained optimistic through several operations, inspiring her daughter, Bonnie, also seriously injured. Margaret was astonished at the stack of get-well cards and the freezer full of hot dishes she found when she got home, disregarding how much of her time had always been spent helping others.

One of the most visible—and audible—women in our community was married to my father's brother Harold. Aunt Josephine spat nails when I talked about the Equal Rights Amendment, but she kept her own brand and separate checking account. She owned cattle, but in cow country, she also owned sheep. "Government supports," she muttered when I asked. "Sheep always make money." The yard was always full of geese and turkeys, no matter how loudly Harold swore about the messes he stepped in with new boots. As a child, she'd helped raise younger siblings and done a man's work; her father preferred the smoky lights of town to country darkness.

She hadn't worked much formal education into her schedule, but when she decided the rural electric cooperative was being mismanaged, she took action. Going to meetings, she asked questions and wrote letters that made executives squirm and change their ways. She took art lessons and painted watercolor scenes of the ranch whenever she got the chance. She organized the OAO (Our Afternoon Off) Club. Anyone needing a potluck dish or money for a worthy cause dialed Jo's telephone number. When neighbors entered the hospital, she rallied women to clean their homes; many an ailing woman miraculously recovered after considering what Jo might find—and talk about—in her refrigerator.

Childless, Jo always had someone else's children in the house. She loved to ride, and she taught children by slinging them on a horse and galloping ahead. Sometimes she walked with toddlers to gather eggs; when they got older, she sent them out with a beat-up bucket to face her huge White Leghorn rooster and his two-inch spurs. Visiting once, I saw two neighbor kids climbing the drainpipe to her roof; Jo shrieked outrage that scrambled them back down, trembling. I'd like to ask if that yell warped their psyches, but as adults they left the county and never came back.

Jo planted windbreak trees around the buildings and corrals and maintained a huge garden. She filled three freezers and hundreds of canning jars every year, and still gave away enough produce to feed a village. No one ever left her house without a meal, or at least coffee and a choice of two kinds of pie and three breeds of cake. Even after they could afford hired help, Jo often worked outside with Harold, but when he came inside, dinner was ready even if he was two hours late and she'd helped brand two hundred calves. Heaven help the hired man who didn't check the heifers every two hours all night during calving season; Jo got up and slipped out in the dark to be sure the job was getting done.

For years, Jo's feet often swelled and bled as a result of some ailment I never understood. She wore loose loafers and walked on her ankles; once in a while she "doped" her feet, but she never mentioned pain. She died hard and slow from a brain tumor.

Margaret planted a tree in my Aunt Jo's memory, fencing it so the cows wouldn't break it down. The spring following her car accident, Margaret planted five hundred windbreak trees and wrote a book about tree-planting on the prairie; her research demonstrated that she knew more about it than the experts she had consulted. By the time she died of the HIV secreted in blood she'd received after her accident, she knew more about AIDS than some experts and spent her last months warning our isolated community. She wasn't in favor of the ERA, either, but her daughter Bonnie is an independent young woman who makes her own tracks.

Jo and Margaret represented generations older and younger than mine, respectively; both epitomized western women, as Margaret's daughter Bonnie is our future. They all encompassed contradictions; working as men's equals, they refused to label themselves "liberated." Strong and independent, they all grew up with men whose habit it was to belittle women. Their work quietly proved such men wrong, but they carried no banners. They knew when to let a man help them. Josephine was famous for gossiping, but when a neighbor was in trouble, she used every scrap of her energy to help; Margaret advised me I need not mention the Equal Rights Amendment when her brother was digging my four-wheel-drive truck out of a snowdrift. Cooperating with the men in my life, I discovered, was not only more tactful at times, but enjoyable; partners accomplished more than competitors. When George and I cut wood for winter, he ran the chain saw; I exercised my abilities stacking the wood. After he died, I gave the chain saw to a woman who already knew how to operate it safely.

What, I wondered in my journals, made these ranch women different from the ones I'd known when I went to college in a city? Certainly part of the contrast was physical and mental toughness. A ranch child sees birth and death before she is six years old; most of us understand the connection between sex and birth before our own bodies prompt us to ask our mothers, who lie anyway. We learn responsibility by doing particular chores, tailored to our size and strength. We appreciate our value in our families as an appendage of the work we do even when city schoolmates laugh at the manure on our boots.

Copying our parents, we shrug when spring blizzards kill so many calves we have to wear last year's school shoes and buy used clothes. We struggle until we can finally lift a heavy saddle straight to the back of our own horses. We discover how intelligence can substitute for strength; riding up to a tight gate with no man in sight, we figure out how the fence stretcher or a rope will loosen it. We find solitude on a warm afternoon, watching from horseback a hawk wheel in a sky far from highways. After mastering the arts of cooking and cleaning in obedience to our mothers, we do our outside chores at dusk, thinking of the choice that is ours.

During the liberation battle in the cities, I concluded that prairie women relish a freedom largely unknown elsewhere, and I applied the lessons Jo and Margaret taught me to living as well as to writing. Writing in South Dakota as the women's movement developed in distant places, I noticed its effect on the women around me; as my pride in my matriarchs grew, I began to relish their differences from women who lacked their opportunities.

None of the women I knew were unusual. Back when the pioneers in this neighborhood were too busy surviving to bother about "gender roles," they developed qualities we currently deprecate as part of the "western myth." Hindsight is a luxury we, unlike the old-timers, can afford. Peculiar, isn't it? The qualities a cowboy developed on the frontier made him a hero in popular culture, while the woman beside him was ignored. She rode West with him, worked and fought beside him; she cooked his meals and bore his children, and she still does. But most little girls don't want to grow up to be cowgirls. Or writers. Hardly had I realized why my neighbors were different before I acknowledged how their admirable qualities could help me survive, writing what I must.

But New York writers still flew, expenses paid, to North Dakota for three days to write articles about abused farm women.

During the early 1980s, I read my father's agricultural papers, supplementing my everyday knowledge with the views of agricultural experts. These professionals—living mostly in college towns in farming regions— urged ranchers to study world markets and modernize their operations with machinery. News stories suggested the family ranch was being replaced by more efficient corporate ranches owned by out-of-state or foreign interests. Environmental publications scolded ranchers for overgrazing public lands to produce nasty beef that would kill consumers by plugging their arteries and giving them cancer. At environmental meetings, I listened politely while animal rights activists yelped about ranchers torturing calves for entertainment and vocal vegetarians proclaimed beef politically incorrect in a starving world.

My father grumbled as he folded each paper and headed for the garage to put new spark plugs in his 1950 John Deere tractor. He grew angrier each year, insisting that the only way to do things was his way. At last George began to study for a degree in counseling; he could not stand to be a rancher under those conditions. When he was ready, I promised, we'd leave the ranch together.

Meanwhile, we stayed. Like the older ranch women around me, I learned to smile and wash potatoes real fast when six unexpected guests showed up at mealtime. I still cared for cows and fixed fences; with George's help, I branded and shoveled snow. We both cooked, and he helped me keep the house reasonably tidy. We slid into country traditions, cussing weathermen who try to predict snow by consulting a machine.

When I wasn't reading to augment my knowledge and perspective, I wrote fiction centered on ranching, most of it quickly rejected. A Florida magazine editor suggested a story set in the branding corral was "unbelievable." I was perplexed; the experience was my own, nothing changed but the names. I began to doubt my ranch realities would ever appear in print. On good days, I imagined my journals providing clues to subsistence on the plains after the next world war wiped out agribusiness along with all the other huge, unwieldy corporate monsters.

But I inherited a stubborn streak; my grandmother Cora Belle Hey regularly killed rattlesnakes and once whacked a skunk to death—with her hoe. Using the diaries I'd kept for years to aid my recall of particularly harrowing events, I began to record our daily lives on a one-family ranch. Even if my writing became nothing more than quaint historical record, it would provide testimony to the way my own ancestors and thousands of my contemporaries on the plains created a ranching civilization. I organized the manuscript like a journal, recording what I did and thought every day. As the writing progressed, I perceived another theme: the stories of women like Jo and Margaret who *chose* ranch life among numerous other options.

An agent in New York had expressed interest in my fiction; after reading part of the journal, she wrote, "The sense that I have from the entries of the sample month is that life on the ranch is so relentlessly hard and tied to the routine of the daily chores involved in the struggle for survival that it would be difficult to sustain a reader's interest for the duration of a book." Even though I've always believed New Yorkers lack most of the qualities I find admirable in plains folk, I was daunted enough to consider writing no more. That same week I saw *Heartland*, about pioneer homesteader Elinore Pruitt Stewart. I walked out of the most authentic film I'd ever seen determined to keep writing, whether a single word was ever printed or not.

I sent samples to every other publisher I thought had any interest in rural life; after twenty-six rejection letters, Barn Owl Books in Berkeley, California, accepted the manuscript. The publisher, Gina Covina, and I mailed the manuscript back and forth for three years before we were both satisfied with it. Both my husband, George, and my friend Margaret became part of my story. I wrote about the aftereffects of the radiation and chemotherapy that cured George's Hodgkin's disease but left him with a dead thyroid; I recorded details of the car accident that injured Margaret and her daughter Bonnie. *Windbreak: A Woman Rancher on the Northern Plains* was published in early 1987, to favorable reviews in the *New York Times Book Review* and elsewhere. I wrote the New York agent to sympathize, sure that she, like me, must be used to mistakes.

Soon, letters from readers began arriving, many addressed only to "Linda Hasselstrom, writer, Hermosa, South Dakota." When Margaret saw me reading one at the mailbox one day, sobbing, she said, "If you're gonna cry that hard, go out in our alfalfa field; we need moisture." Ranch women— and men—young and old scrawled their thanks to me for chronicling their lives. From Michigan came a letter from a woman who drove a bus for a living, longing to move West and raise horses; with her husband—her best friend, she wrote—she lived in a log cabin with a hand pump and wood stove in the kitchen, fifteen miles from town. A hunting camp cook thanked me for helping her get through long nights when male hunters bragged and drank. Ranchers retired to California wrote movingly of their own pioneering lives.

Old friends who'd always wondered what happened to me when I quit studying for my Ph.D. and headed back to the ranch wrote to congratulate me on becoming rich and famous. A few years before, they'd predicted I'd hate the grim life of hardship and toil; now they wanted to vacation on the ranch next summer. A Wisconsin musician whose engineer wife works in town sent me some cheese from their goats and asked how I juggled my two contrasting roles. He wrote that when he walked "into chamber music rehearsals wearing big overalls with cello in hand, many people have trouble with my mixing 'uniforms.' In contrast, friends down at the feed mill seem more accepting of my other roles, including my favorite as 'house daddy.'"

A woman wrote from California's San Joaquin Valley that I had taken her home to Nebraska, and an elderly woman sent me a photo of her apartment above a New Jersey garage and thanked me for making it the wide open spaces for a while. Several told me of their loneliness on the ranch as their children moved on and their husbands died; I'd expressed clearly, they said, why they chose to stay. Teenagers who yearned to raise goats on a little acreage in the country sent me their photos and phone numbers; while some thanked me for showing them stark reality, others were headed West to become my apprentices, and one man proposed. City-bound vegetarians scribbled of how they worried about my cows when the local weatherman described Great Plains blizzards. Some country women allowed as how this writing business wasn't so hard; they'd kept diaries all their lives and now I could help them publish, so they could be rich and famous too. Many people asked about Margaret and George, or wished them well.

For nearly a year, I answered every letter, almost four hundred, personally; I answered questions and encouraged diarists to give copies of their histories to their children and to historical archives. I began to believe that many qualities I appreciate in western women are potentially present in others; prairie life makes them manifest in a different way, but folks who ride subways in New York may be as guardedly alert as any plains Army Scout of 1861.

Finally, as letter-writing consumed more time than writing or ranching, I composed a computerized reply; to date, the letters number more than seven hundred. I saw the need to save time but mourned even as I but relished the words of friends I'd never meet. *Windbreak* multiplied my opportunities for work and further publication. A second book, *Going Over East: Reflections of a Woman Rancher*, was published late that same year. Colleges offered me further distractions from writing: money to speak about writing and the environment. Abruptly, I saw myself representing a breed many people didn't know existed: the western woman. Hesitant about speaking for the cantankerous women I knew, I also believed we needed to be recognized as part of the West as well as the environmental movement. All of us form an unofficial alliance marching out of the past into an indefinite future; we are neighbors in the original sense, as I learned from Margaret: "Your friend on the next farm."

My father, however, was furious; I'd broken two principal rules by referring to him, accurately, as my stepfather, and by writing about our lives on the ranch. He'd revealed a rancher's standards as our horses trotted side by side: Show no pain. Our business is no one else's. Introspection is a luxury, self-analysis a sign of weakness or dementia. Now he groused, "If you've gotta write, find something to doodle about besides me and this ranch."

Late in 1987, I received a carbon copy of a letter written by a reader to a major romance publisher; in the letter she complained that the novel she'd just finished reading had been largely copied from *Windbreak*. "The unwritten rule of horsemanship is never to hold on to the saddle horn in front of witnesses," I'd written, adding, "George insists my saddle horn has teeth marks in it where I tried to get an extra grip when holding on with both hands wasn't working."

The romance writer had typed,

> "The first rule of riding is never to grab the saddle pommel in front of witnesses," Tom Malcolm told Shyloh. "But Rand doesn't count. His saddle pommel has teeth marks in it from when holding on with both hands wasn't enough."

I read the letter to George as we sat, weary from moving cows, in a little café in Hermosa during the summer of 1988. We laughed; what the other writer called "pommel" is the saddle's "swell," under the horn. But as I read other parallel passages quoted by the irate reader my stomach twisted as it did the time I was hospitalized after throwing up for twenty-four hours straight.

The romance writer had stolen my father's life and my love for George, tricked my words out in tawdry cosmetics.

One book in a projected series of three had already appeared on newsstands; the second was printed, and the third existed in manuscript. I found material closely matching mine in all three.

My publisher hired a lawyer; litigation resulted in a settlement, announced on Christmas Eve: a cash award of roughly half the cash payment the romance writer received for the first book. The second was shredded without going on sale, and the third was rejected. All that time, I kept asking myself one question, never answered: How could any writer steal another writer's words? It was my first gut-level understanding that not everyone was serious about writing in the way I am.

Halfway through the lawsuit, George died of a malignant spinal tumor caused by the radiation that had helped cure his Hodgkin's disease. Ten days elapsed between our discovery that the pain in his shrunken shoulder was a malignancy and the day he was buried in the little cemetery on a bare hillside a few miles from home. He was forty-two years old.

Many people who had written to me about *Windbreak* learned of his death and wrote to me again to remind me how strong the woman named Linda is in that book. People robbed by death assured me that I could survive this desolation. Once I understood, I knew the real message of our tradition, older than wagon tracks on the plains; I'd matured into a ranch woman.

Twice, far out in a pasture, I have seen a dark column rise out of the pale buffalo grass. Water and DNA flow in spirals, as do sound and light, and tornadoes. It's a dust devil, I thought. Or perhaps a bolt of pure energy ascending from earth to sky. Or the opposite: galaxies auguring star power into the ground. Magic. Angels coming to rescue or revenge.

Closer to the swirling shape, I was still puzzled. No one had plowed this prairie; even a plains wind couldn't lift such dust through this primordial grass. Finally, my eyes focused on hundreds of birds flying in circles. Together, they formed a whirling shaft mounting the air: a hawk spiral. Birdwatchers who visit the prairie tell me such sightings are rare; in fifty years of living on the plains, I've seen hawk spirals only twice.

I lay down on a little knoll, counting birds until I grew dizzy. The earth was warm; long grass blew over me like ocean swells. Hundreds of wings whipped the air; closing my eyes, I visualized torrents of wind flowing outward from this center, covering the earth. The air pouring into my lungs was power-charged.

As hawks whirled slowly overhead, I memorized markings and shapes in flight to look up ones I didn't know. Red-tailed hawks revolved around ferruginous and rough-legged hawks; merlins and kestrels skittered between. A peregrine falcon sailed the edges of the circle.

I picked one red-tailed hawk to watch through a monocular as he flew straight into the base of the whirlwind. First he circled low, as if hunting, but each revolution took him higher; in a dozen rounds, he was halfway up the column of birds. In ten more minutes, he blasted out the top of the hoop and glided west, hunting. He drifted back and forth over a ridge until he paused, wings fluttering, and dropped on something in the grass. Experts say that when hawks do this they are playing, showing off their skills for a specialized audience of other winged predators. Hawks spiral only when they migrate, traveling from one homeland—one part of their vast personal terrain—to another.

The universe loops around and around again, repeating itself in perfect circles. Sometimes we watch the same story over and again until we understand.

My forty-ninth birthday came three years after George died. That night, I dreamed of opening a shallow, clean box filled with bones; I knew by their length that these were George's arms and legs. I wept, lifting the skeletons of his big hands, rubbing my fingertips over their coarse texture. He always apologized for his rough skin, but his touch was gentle. Tenderly, I placed each bone on a wool blanket we took when we went camping.

As I arranged the fragments, my rational mind intruded to remind me that the skeleton inside George's coffin would not be immaculate. Even cattle carcasses cleaned by vultures and coyotes in plains weather retain bits of ragged sinew and rotten flesh. I heard scornful laughter in a hollow skull. *She's avoiding reality again.*

The sweet bone-gathering dream switched off, and I flew through the air wearing a sturdy harness around my chest, waist, legs, and ankles. For a moment I admired a carnival as I dangled above it, secure and unafraid. The pressure of the straps increased; I soared higher, sweeping through a great crescent.

Rrrrrip! A Velcro fastening parted. I looked down; a strap around one ankle trailed loose. One by one, the straps ruptured as I watched: my ankles were free, then my legs, my waist. Only straps around my chest held me, so tight I wheezed. Gravity at the end of my next arc would snatch them open; I would spin out beyond the stars.

In May of 1992 I left the ranch, temporarily I thought; I took our West Highland terrier, Frodo, and a few writing supplies to Jerry's house five hours away, close enough to return quickly in the emergency I expected as my father's mind and health failed. For income, I rented to strangers the house George and I had built. Every week, I raced back and forth between the ranch and Wyoming's capital city. Frodo balanced on a sleeping bag and books in the back of my Bronco, whining at familiar smells. We stopped to stroll through cemeteries and along highway ditches. After years of fastening my roots in prairie sod, I'd become a modern nomad.

My father died on August 7, 1992, a month after my dream of whirling into space, five months before my best friend Margaret's death. A week after my father's funeral, I took mother to see their lawyer and she learned how many acres he owned; I'd looked it up on the tax rolls. I'd inherited nothing, but father's bequest to mother proved so large that even she faced ruinous taxes and asked my help. During two years of legal work I found land deeds in a damp cellar and records of my father's investments scattered among rafters in the basement and lock boxes in the house. Nearly everything was in his name alone; only lawyers and accountants could unravel the quagmire he'd created by trusting no one.

A real-estate appraiser came one day to look at the leaning barn and sagging corrals. Tabulating rolls of new wire and posts stacked along drooping pasture fences, he noted antiquated tractors and trucks and piles of old machinery parts. Leaving, he said solemnly, "I guess your dad practiced what we in the real-estate business call 'deferred maintenance.'"

My mother owns her house and barns, along with dozens of investments managed by a trust. Confined to a nursing home by osteoporosis, she is happily revising her memories.

I have touched down in a city; Jerry and I are buying an old house, but I own the ranch. Mother sold my father's cattle herd to pay probate costs. I sold my cows and borrowed money to pay property taxes and buy the land.

With little money for repairs my father was unable to do after George died, I leased the land to a neighbor. His hired man lives in the house where I grew up.

When I discussed my choices with my Uncle Max, he wept. "You worked all your life to have that ranch and cattle; now you have to sell the cows to try to hang on to the land," he said. "It's not right. What in hell was wrong with my brother?"

Joan Didion says, "I think nobody owns land until their dead are in it." By that standard, I'm authorized to my fragment of prairie, but I have always distrusted absentee ownership. Sometimes, reviewing my diaries from past years, I discover an understanding from the 1970s that I duplicated in the 1980s, mastering life's lessons slowly, if at all. Often I am horrified by my own revelations, tempted to retreat behind the barricade of family secrecy traditional on the plains.

Shortly after George died, I read from my work at an agricultural college in the eastern farming region of South Dakota. One teacher asked students to write down their comments and sent me my favorite; my mother, if she could understand, would be gratified that her predictions were accurate.

"She seemed," wrote the young man, "to be like the boots she had on, worn and broken-in to hardship but, because of that, soft, supple, and beautiful."

The Maternity Wing, Madison, Minnesota

Carol Bly

The simpler the animal, the stronger its sense of place. In all their lives, miniature monkeys do not venture beyond the five or six trees of their babyhood. No matter how diligently the Department of Natural Resources live-catches and relocates them, tough old mama beavers devote themselves, successfully, too, to getting back to the familiar lodge. You need not be intelligent to love a place: that natural emotion comes freely to us all. Love of place is an extrovert's emotion: for one thing, it is nothing if not particular, and its point of concentration is something visible—*these* stars, for example, not the Southern Cross; *this* prairie of stiff grasses, not the feral relief of the Andes; or these trees or this building at a particular north latitude and degree of west longitude. Love of place is no part of that invisible kit that St. Paul called "the whole armor of God," which he advised people to put on. Love of place is not what liberal-arts education is about. Love of place is nearly, not quite, irrelevant to the two most marvelous qualities of our species: first, our idea that mercy is a good thing, even when it is practiced toward people whom it is not profitable to be merciful to; and second, our belief that being just to people is a good thing, even when it doesn't do

Copyright 1995 by Carol Bly

us any benefit. Justice, in fact, is all the more to the purpose when it is exercised for those who cannot slug it out for themselves to get what's fair. That group includes newborn babies and men less heavily armed than other men, small governments situated at the edge of large governments, women who choose not to arm themselves heavily, most children, most old people, and *everybody*, even the bullies, of future generations who can't stand up to us about the poisoned or denuded earth we leave for them.

Mercy and justice are reasons to love our species, however poorly we practice them. At least we have the idea, which is more than you can say for snakes or even lions. I love us for that. I don't love our species because we have fond feelings for particular places—a backyard near the forty-seventh parallel or some road an aunt walked on, or in my case just now, the maternity wing of the Madison (Minnesota) Hospital. In fact, being crazy about some remembered place is a dumb emotion.

Dumb emotion or not, I have it. I love a number of particular places and want to think about one of them, the maternity wing of a small town's hospital. But this essay is also about how some people get liberal-arts educations and some people don't. I have had that kind of education called the liberal arts. Its major principle is that you practice turning mere *things* into *thought.* That's the idea of it!—to get things into their basic crystalline form, to feel their structure inside yourself, to lay down any sword you happen to be carrying because you have memorized the *idea* of swords and internalized the good of swords if there is some good to them. Liberal-arts educated people prefer essence to surface every time. They boast nearly constantly, too. Socrates and Epictetus started the Western world boasting about contemplation, boasting about making assays of things, boasting about reflecting on them. Like extroverted hobbyists, Socrates and Epictetus commended their kind of thinking to others. Good thing for them, just as it is for people who push other people into learning crocheting, that our species is dead keen on getting advice. I am continually surprised by how carefully we listen to wild counsel from one another. Still, there are limits. Most of us feel disdainful of St. Paul's contumely and his overconfident way of telling us what to do; I can barely imagine going up to friends and saying, "I suggest you put on the whole armor of God."

It has to be said for place-lovers: they do not boast as much as theory lovers. E. B. White's "Once Again to the Lake" is annoying because he goes on about a place where only the very rich could ever go, but he doesn't boast of it or counsel us to build million-dollar portfolios so that we, too, might go there. I have never heard people boast about love of place. They don't say, "Listen, I love my field with its organic loam more profoundly than you love your cottonwood's shadow in the moonlight." I expect we pro-thought types boast for two reasons: first, we want attention since we tend to be low on money, and second, we do deeply feel that memorizing life as it floats by makes for happiness. We want everyone in on that happiness.

Memorizing life as it goes by is the peculiar habit of a liberal-arts education. This habit says, in a rough parallel, "Get everything into documents and folders! Back up everything on disk. Carry many uninitialized disks in your pockets." We memorizers tend to memorize not only *good* places like the Madison Hospital but lesser experiences as well—enemies' remarks and scrappy comparisons between one person's idea of God and another's—a truly stupid quarrel, as Whitman said outright. Memorizers pick up and memorize lesser stuff along with any original hypotheses they make. Because they deliberately cultivate the habit of "internalizing," as psychologists say, they internalize unearned admiration of themselves and they internalize old emotional responses, and, worst of all, they internalize cultural junk—such as the class system. I mean the psychological class system, the habit of seeing some people as greater, others as lesser. I want to tell about my internalizing of some cultural junk and how it affected me in the nice hospital where I gave birth to four children.

The Madison Hospital was and no doubt still is a small, unbelievably friendly small-town hospital. The town is some twenty miles from the South Dakota border, about one hundred sixty-five miles due west of Minneapolis. I liked having babies. I used to wake several times each night, once or twice to breast-feed the baby, once or twice to take fruit juice from the nursing staff. They were up and about all night anyhow, making themselves toast somewhere far down the hall, checking on critically ill people, letting me hold my baby longer than is usual policy. I told myself, again and again,

"Memorize this wonderful place and this wonderful time of life so it will be *inside* you and you will not feel bereft when the baby is grown and you are old, even all-the-way old, doing the inescapable, solitary work of dying."

At night a stroke victim gave his rhythmic cries for hours. I called softly to the licensed practical nurse. She came squeaking along on her rubber-soled shoes. I asked whether they couldn't give something to whoever was in pain. I had such gall: how could I make such a suggestion unless I took myself for more sensitive, more humane, than she? Ridiculous. Still, the thrum of that fellow's cries got into me the way vibration gets into any tinny object.

"He's not in pain," she explained. "He is *trying* to die." I decided to memorize that, too: two brand-new human beings lay in bassinets or in their mothers' arms, while someone else was trying and trying to do that part of life we call the death.

"You will not always be in the maternity wing," I told myself, a little fiercely, because I was afraid of death, "cossetted by the staff, preferred, even, to other mothers because you are breast-feeding, not bottle-feeding, your child; some day you must gear up to do as chipper and considerate job of dying as you can." I memorized that to myself, and then went off the subject, since a little character-building thinking went a long way. At that time I liked the psychologically slack business of self-congratulation over having had a baby.

The Madison Hospital has huge picture windows. At night on the prairie, of course, but even in the town, which was so small it didn't spoil the night with its lights, the scarf of stars slowly pulled across the sky. My first child was born in January, so the sky looked profoundly cold and more than ever unconnected to human beings. All those tons of fire—the stars—do not love *our* gravity field at all; they do not care about *our* place. They wordlessly obey their own bosses out there. They are programmed to race farther and farther apart from one another, cooling, collapsing, exploding, and starting the whole lot again. It is nothing to them whether we name their births twelve thousand million light-years away or not. I held my first baby for hours, trying to feel affectionate to those far spaces. It was no good. I only wanted to make a warm place for my baby with walls to keep out the cold stars and I wanted her not to die until she was so old she would want it. It was such a queer thing—feeling the hot new baby, feeling judgmental about the stars and the night because they were indifferent to me (there is nothing like indifference to wake up the judgmental instincts of a judgmental person anyhow) and commiserating with the stroke patient.

Late on my first full day, a powerful woman, just then the only other mother in the hospital, shuffled and scraped her way into my room. "You want visitors?" she asked. But she was already in. "They never leave my baby with me that long." She gave mine an unexpressive glance.

A nurse came in with a tray of wildly tinted drinks—cranberry cocktail (who knows what chemicals have been tucked into that stuff), orange juice of the canned kind, grapefruit juice. I took one of everything.

"How come she gets all them?" the other mother said.

The nurse raised her face in a canny mix of balefulness and dignity. "She," she said, with unmistakable emphasis, "is a nursing mother."

There it was—greater people and lesser people, the American two-class system, albeit a pastel version—merely breast-feeder vs. bottle-giver. Behind breast-feeding versus bottle-feeding, however, lay another up/down paradigm: educated people vs. uneducated people.

Someone has to be *down*, so the others can feel more *up*. I bring this up because I loved the Madison Hospital, but the American class system was astir in it the way beetles and rats are astir in a ship's hold. Those of us who believe in the liberal-arts sort of education are always advising ourselves and others to *internalize* this or that: memorize this moment! memorize this place! We are the originators of that expression travelers use: taking it *in*. "Been to Paris?" "Yup, took in Paris all right. Berlin, too. Utah Beachhead." We incidentally internalize the two-class way of thinking along with the other ideas. Up/down thinking sometimes floods in with the good ideas like mercy and justice the way a whale's mouthful of seawater takes not only those fish the whale had in mind but a few thousand other sour-tasting fellows, lower on the food chain, who slop right in, too.

In animals we call a two-class system a "pecking order." In us we call it "primitive feelings of entitlement" and several other names. Whatever we call it, it is awfully low on the thought chain. Like whales, however, we toss it back.

Like any woman of my generation, I was used to that particular psychological evil. In 1962, non-college-educated males looked *down* on women. A good many college-educated ones did, too. I knew what it was to be in the *down* group. I knew it was such a prevalent evil I couldn't expect even so kindly a place as the maternity wing of the Madison Hospital to be free of it. Two-class thinking was, hey!—reality. I wouldn't even mention it except that I only recently identified a specific genus of two-class thinking that I had brought into the hospital inside myself.

The Madison Hospital was free of any other pyschological ills. In the 1960s, a time when hospitals were abandoning their identity as loving institutions, the Madison Hospital went on serving patients with extraordinary kindliness. TV often stereotypes hospital administrators as ogres. Ours was not an ogre. He was nothing like the 1960s zombies who licked up new tricks from the Harvard Business School. Our administrator was half crow's-nest lookout and half convoy commander. Like a sailor who has the watch, he guarded against under-the-surface threats from the outside. His enemies were certain, but not all, federal legislation, certain, but not all, pressures from insurance companies, the litigious nature of American society itself—and the new, frightening demographic changes. He kept the hospital's mission flexible the way a convoy commander has to be ready to change zigzag. He managed "by walking around" as the authors of *In Search of Excellence* made so much of. He visited those of us in the maternity wing. He did not duck clear of the dying and their relatives. What's more, his hospital treated anyone ill or wounded. Thirty years later, a farmhand told me that she could not have a deteriorating knee looked after because she could not afford insurance. In the 1960s, the poorest farm help or unemployed person in Lac qui Parle County got treatment at the hospital. The hospital was kind. At the gross level, the American class system was scarcely shown there. One could miss it the way one might not notice an unlabeled bottle that stands motionless on a shelf alongside bottles of useful medicines.

I was in the *up* group of the maternity wing, not just because I breast-fed babies when the other new mothers didn't, but because my husband and I were educated. Not only was my husband educated, but he brought me roses and presents. The nurses praised my baby, while they scarcely looked at the rough-spoken mother whose new baby lay in the bassinet next to mine.

That other mother had a curious look about her. Her skin was opaque. It looked more like coarse-woven cloth than skin, giving off no light—like burlap. One of the nurses, often finding her standing at the foot of my bed, would brush by her and say "Excuse *me*" with the accent on the *me*. (That pronunciation says, "It is you who need to apologize, not I.") The paternity of at least her first child was a question that had regaled coffee klatches some years earlier. She then married. She had a great many babies after that. More important, she was a poor person. When the rich people of our town had children out of wedlock, it was not forgotten but the effect was a glint of glamour about the mother, not disgrace. This woman was ten or twelve thousand dollars a year too poor to qualify for that category. What's more, her husband "put her in the field," as we called it: that is, she helped with the farming as well as did the household chores and child rearing. Her heavy skin was the gift of wind and the rub of dirt. Her grammar was like most bad usage: a series of shy, courageous, unfocused approximations— snatches of phrases, sometimes a single word shot out like a stone from a slingshot. Sometimes her tone of voice reminded me of the comic magazines of my childhood, in which Germans in enemy uniform were forever shouting *Verboten!* at one another. (We who were kids in the 1940s had a working Nazi accent we could pull out for gags.) Some of this mother's exclamations were like those hoarse explosions.

Psychotherapists and clinical social workers have a reason for asking us to speak fully, *in whole sentences*: only complete sentences contain exactitude, not guesswork. If we are lucky, someone taught us in school or in therapy to speak whole sentences. Conversely, psychologically or culturally unlucky people have a damnable time making a real sentence: they haven't the confidence for it. "Oh!" they cry. "Doctors! Show me a doctor and I'll show you . . ." They have strong feelings—hatreds, admirations, memories—and would like to express them—but they also have a profound need *not* to express them because the listener might be scornful. What they are hurting from, and stymied by, is *cultural abuse*. Therefore, they say unclear *halves* of statements and then look at you opaquely, so that you will *not* see in: they are afraid you will locate something in there and shoot at it.

The other mother came into my hospital room a lot. She didn't particularly want to talk about labor, but she was willing to because I was obviously interested in it. She gradually told me that she didn't cotton to labor and delivery. She didn't cotton to breast-feeding, either. We had to dodge around, she and I, for topics to talk about. I was madly enthusiastic about my doctor, but hers had disappointed her somehow. She did not cotton to him, she told me, but in bits. In fragments, gradually, she told me she did not cotton to the nurses too much either. "I don't know," she said. Then she said in an including and friendly way, "Well, you know . . . !"

I was not the conversationalist I am now. I have always been fond of filthy language, but I hadn't such a dirty tongue in my head back then. I steered clear of her, all those things and people she didn't cotton to. *Now* if I listened to that woman, as she prowled about the foot of my hospital bed, once shyly putting such work-hardened fingers to the roses that I bet she could not feel the instant when the petals touched her skin—*now* I would respect her enough to ask her a question about the very subject she most wanted to talk about. I would ask her conversationally, "What do you think is the most jack shit thing in the world?"

For a split second people freeze at such a question, but then their faces break open like splendid shards of mica "What do I think is the most jack shit thing in the world? What do I think is—! Do you want to really know what it is? It's—" and the room fills with clarity. You can practically watch the clarity and warmth filling the room. Of course, such a question would empty the room of tricky posturing and let it fill with clarity and warmth. The questioner has risked sounding both foolish and vulgar. In our up/down world, the listener gains confidence by comparison—and feels trusting, if not respectful. A parallel: Let us say that we are campers who have taken shelter in a cave. Relaxed, indolent snakes lie around here and there, moving along in the cracks and behind our pile of rucksacks. Then there is an intervention. The word is, everything tricky and chill, get out. All of the snakes start easing along toward the cave entrance. There is a gratifying moment when the last two leave, making their tandem wriggles in that alien way. Now the cave fills up with large, nonaggressive, fur-bearing animals, mammals like us. They plunge in, ranging around, sniffing, yawning, some of them growling and deliberately barging into one another with their heads, so that they lose balance and have to rebrace themselves on their huge feet. From a sojourner's point of view these mammals are not ideal but they are an improvement over snakes.

But I didn't think to ask the other mother anything. I was passive. I had my own responsibilities, and they felt holy to me. After all, a new child lay on my breast. I had sung to her "Maxwelton's Braes Are Bonny" (Annie Laurie) and "Auld Lang Syne" and "The Skye Boat Song" because I am a Scottish-American, and "Jeg Er Så Glad Hver Juli Kvell" and "Ja, Vi Elsker Dette Landet" because her father is a Norwegian-American. The baby's tiny ear wasn't two feet from my mouth. I knew enough not to inquire, right above a baby's ear, "What do you think is the most jack shit thing in the world?"

The other mother settled for gossip about the big shots in town. How she had been treated by them was her subject. But first she had to make certain I wasn't one of them. Any fool could tell I was educated—bad. On the other hand, everyone knew that my husband and I had neither television nor "water up to the house" (indoor plumbing)—good. She and I felt our way from very-small talk to medium-small talk to actually engaging talk. Eventually she made the observation that was and is a central bugbear to me: human beings will give up everything before they will give up their position in the pecking order.

From time to time one nurse or another would tell me that if I was tired I could call and they'd close my door so "people" didn't "just wander in." They meant the other mother—whom else? Several times they told me my baby was "just beautiful, just beautiful." In the late afternoon of my first day in the hospital I tottered down the hall to have a look at both babies. I noticed something fascinating: the other mother's baby was beautiful, too. It had fine features for someone only three days old. It had gorgeous curly hair, a lot of it. The next time a nurse brought me my baby and praised it, I told her that that other baby was utterly beautiful, too.

"All babies are cute," the nurse said, "but yours is a doll."

"That other one is beautiful," I repeated.

"You let me know if you want anything," the nurse replied. There it was.

This *it*, the up/down philosophy, had shown up in the delivery room at four-fifteen in the morning as well. My first child's birth was straightforward and comparatively easy. In 1962 mothers got a shot of Demerol during labor, and when doing the final work of delivering the baby we got a whiff of gorgeous stuff called Trilene. In the delivery room were people dear to me: my sister-in-law, who was a licensed practical nurse; the family doctor; and two RNs who floated in and out of my notice partly because I was busy enough and partly because they were attending to a patient in the main part of the hospital who was in critical condition. When someone laid the baby, with its white and red splotches, on my stomach, I got very high. Then one of the RNs, a new person there, leaned over me and said, "Now—isn't this the best experience of your life?"

I was boundlessly ecstatic, so I would have agreed with anything anyone said. I was just about to cry "O yes! Yes! It is!" when I took note of an oddly intense expression in her face. The nurse was regarding me powerfully, not passively: her face hung right over mine. She was not *asking* me for my answer—she seemed to be *willing* me to say yes. I took warning. Something lay under the surface here—O yes, in the next second I thought I knew what it was: the nurse wanted me to sell out my life as an intellectual and thirty-one-year-old free-thinker! She wanted me to say that giving birth to offspring—which anyone knows rats and rabbits do fifty-two times faster and four times more often than we do—she wanted me to say that that was *better* than all the alternately grave and merry and complicated doings of the mind and heart. I could hear it in her tone. She wanted me to sell human beings short.

Well, I would have to stand up for the mind. I felt myself trembling and self-satisfied, a latter-day Nathan Hale as satisfied with my cause as he was with his.

"No," I crowed up at her. "It is lovely but it is not the greatest experience of life!"

The nurse's face changed. She squared away, straightened, then vanished. I was free now to enjoy the baby. I decided to do some out-loud meditation, too. I asked the doctor his opinion on several abstruse issues: I knew he was busy over to my left, doing something with the placenta over a slop tray. His hands were still red with my blood. Although taken with that idea a little, I was still too high to stick to any one subject. I told the other nurse some profound things, too. I thought I was a rare treat, intellectually.

Thirty-two years later the woman who had been the new baby told me that after delivery, a mother's body produces chemicals that are like pleasurable drugs—so my springy Weltanschauung that night was just drugs. Oh well.

At last a nurse gave me a ride down the hall on a gurney. It was even more luxurious than the wagon rides of childhood. I had been the baby of my family, with three older brothers. In return for my doing chores or promising not to tell on them, or sometimes simply out of the goodness of their hearts, one brother or another would pull me back uphill in the wagon. It was such swank to feel the cracks of the sidewalk sections thumping underneath and not to have to toil uphill myself. On this gurney ride now, I thought, raising a child will be serious work. This may be the last free ride. You had better memorize this feeling, I said to myself.

Then I lay awake happily. Outside in the January cold, the stars were, as always, indifferent. I felt so happy that I did not mind it that the stars love only themselves, not us, and that no guardian of ours walks their night-soaked paths around the galaxies. It is enough, I thought, to live at all— with luck, the whole three score years and ten.

The next day a blizzard blew its white flanks and empty banners all day, just outside my window. I heard, while choosing a glass of juice to drink, that the doctor had gone off into the country on someone's snowmobile in order to pronounce a death. The driver and he couldn't see to get through and had had to return. Inside our hospital everything was warm. There was less of the hiss of wings, the nurses' tennies, the hall was quiet now, because at last the stroke victim had died. The other mother came to visit when I awoke.

I woke remembering the nurse's odd question: "Now—isn't this the best experience of your life?'' Why should she want me to sell out the life of thinking? Socrates may have thought life without reflection wasn't worth living, but very likely some millions of people hate impractical thinking. They don't quite like people who do think, either.

The other mother came in with her burlap face and heel-less slippers. When my husband was there she would edge out, but give him an appraising look before leaving. I had to guess at her feelings. Her face was like a gunnysack that waits all day on the farmhouse stoop: in the evening, he has promised, ''when he has a chance to get to it,'' the head of the household will do that chore—but for now it waits. Only now and then you see the slightest, most subtle denting or bulge in the burlap, some tiny movement that tells you that the latest litter of kittens is in there waiting.

The other mother did not cotton to most of my conversation. The second day in the hospital I decided I would lick down my baby some. Now it may have gotten to be the in thing in Marin County, California, or in the basement of the Museum of Modern Art, to lick down your babies, but it was not the in thing in the Madison Hospital. When female guests came to visit, I moseyed around the subject to find out if anyone else had done it. I could get no sense of it. I certainly could not say to the other mother, the next time she shuffled in, ''Would you share this—all those babies you've had . . . did you lick any of them down?'' I know that she would not have cottoned to the idea. Vegetarianism has come in, and shamanism has a small following among engineering students now, but I did not then and I still don't think that licking babies all over has caught fire much. I tried to imagine how it would go if I plainly, openly, brought it up. ''Look,'' I rehearsed to myself, imagining the impassive face over the foot of my bed, ''reindeer do it—they do more, actually. They eat the whole placenta, which returns a lot of B vitamins and protein to them . . . so it's natural, you see!''

I knew that that face would not move a millimeter.

I had one other subject to try with her. What did she think about the stroke victim dying in the hospital? She did not know that man. She had no feelings about his death.

''Well, look,'' I wanted to say, ''someone else's death . . . someone else's death is nothing but a kind of universal engine parked on the lay-by track ahead. Our train goes smashing past on the main track. We note that engine stopped there, and go madly forward in our own lives."

Such remarks are an imposition. There is nothing the listener can say unless he or she has the same impression. I would not be surprised if someone listening to someone else talking about a death as an engine on the by-track simply leapt to his feet and swore, "You just shut up about trains! And death, too. Death, too."

I thought the nurse was an enemy of intellectual life. I thought I was a more sensitive listener to the other mother than were the nurses. I was sure I should fight for my right to *think*!

How slowly, how a thousand times slowly, a human being learns anything! My first child was born in 1962, more than thirty-two years ago. Yet only two years ago did I discover what the nurse's expression meant, when she had leaned over me and said, "Now—isn't this the best experience of your life?"

I discovered the meaning of it because an associate of a Twin Cities organization called the Center for Arts Criticism wrote a letter in the center's newsletter. Among her remarks she said that *rural* people should be encouraged to pursue "craftsmanship for its own sake," not real art—not passionate, universal literature. Rural people, she apparently thought, should make quilts and do bookbinding, while the rest of us, the *up* people, get to tackle the great subjects of our species. It was good enough for rural people to spin and knit and carve while we others will try to figure out why it is fun for some human beings to discount the feelings of others, why it gives pleasure to some powerful males and females to torture and kill others, how we could do long-range brainstorming to stop it, why we feel forlorn that the night, so full of dark weight and fires, cares nothing for us. How we can live happily while conscious of death, and choose not to be terrified.

I saw a subtle goal of our species: it is to divide us into those who will be encouraged to meditate and others who will be conditioned not even to want to meditate. Those others, the junk culture tells us, had better learn a craft. All her life, that nurse who bent over me had been told to be practical. When she decided on prenursing for the first two years of her four-year B.S. in nursing, she did it to be practical. Her Sunday School teacher didn't quote to her Shakespeare's line about free choice: "Study, sir, what you most affect."

And like everyone else she knew, I had misread her face. I had been drinking mouthfuls and stomachfuls of the American class system without noticing the taste. Her face had not ordered me to sell out the intellectual life! Her face had said, "I do not want life to be only practical! I want life to be odd—odd and holy—as if we were all connected by invisible cloth."

The nurse's face meant to say, "We human beings feel our way along that cloth. We can't *see* the cloth because it lies in spacious darkness, but we can memorize our ideas about it. First we can memorize the very idea that such cloth is there. I want to know that that is true."

That is what the nurse's face really said, but I mistook it.

Her face said, "In the American class system, some people are never told to memorize an invisible idea."

Her face said, "Please tell me that the American class system is horrible."

It was not really her face that said all these things. It was a slight movement behind her face, a moment's dent in her ordinary expression, and I missed it.

Is Minnesota in America Yet?

Bill Holm

A few years ago, after working myself into a state of high moral dudgeon over one of America's several recent wars, or government-sponsored financial scandals, or servings of one too many dollops of sanctimonious hypocrisy in public speech, I proposed secession to my neighbors in Minneota, even suggesting that our local senator start the legal process of severance in the legislature. Technically, this is treason, I suppose, but Minneotans (like all their fellow Minnesotans), take news of major crimes and catastrophes calmly. It is the small ones—joining the county library, the new wastewater plant, the mileage on the second police car—that push them over into indignation.

"I've had it with Washington," I said righteously. "They take a half-billion cash for defense out of the Second Congressional District and give us Grenada (or Libya, or Panama, etc.). We could defend ourselves for a fraction of that, put a few of the boys from the liquor store on the South Dakota and Iowa borders with a little beer and a case or two of shotgun shells. They'd keep the Grenada militia or Noriega's storm troops safely outside Minneota. Then we could take the half-billion and pay off the farm

Copyright 1995 by Bill Holm

debt. "In fact," I continued from behind my invisible podium, "if we don't declare outright independence and seal the borders at Luverne and Hendricks, we can always join the Canadians. They're having trouble with Quebec, anyway, and could use another province in the south. We'd have civilized health insurance at last, better fishing, and a musically and morally superior anthem." ("O Canada" is, by any standard, an improvement on "The Star-Spangled Banner." It is gentle and singable, with lyrics more full of praise and sweetness than blood and guts.)

After a few long sighs, a roll of the dice for coffee, and a pull or two on a hat brim, I got responses like: "Well, they got that good wheat pool up there; I believe a fellow could do a little better on grain prices then." Or "the beer up there sure is stronger—the Canadians don't go for that 'lite' stuff." Or "my wife's cousin farms up by Brandon. He was laid up with a hernia operation last year—says it didn't cost a thing, and the hospital was real nice." And more . . . In the middle of the chest-thumping patriotic gunboat eighties, I seemed to have uncovered a live strain of secessionist sentiment, plain citizens ready to move the border south, or to declare independence, like a Balkan republic or South Carolina, and get on with the business of daily life, minus Washington. "From sea to shining sea" had shrunk from Big Stone Lake on the Dakota border all the way to Lake Superior.

Are these plain farmers and neighbors poor Americans, or has the process not quite gotten finished inside them? It's one thing to be an external American—just in ceremony, like Charlemagne baptizing the German army by marching it through the Rhine—but what does it mean, in an interior sense, to be American? Has Minnesota joined the union yet, psychologically? The possible answers to these questions may be more interesting and less obvious than we imagine.

Begin with the commonplace notion of Minnesota smugness—the feeling we have that we are somehow cleaner, more virtuous, harder working, better governed, more boring but more civilized than "them," whoever "they" are. Any reader of the essay can think quickly of ten examples of it: in newspapers, political speeches, church sermons, coffee-table talk. Turn on public radio, and you will hear the tune, sometimes a shy counter melody, sometimes tutti-fortissimo . . . It is not our most attractive quality as a state. But is it true?

Partly. Daniel Elazar, in *Cities of the Prairie*, describes Minnesota up to the sixties with uncanny accuracy. He first remarks on the nastiness of Minnesota's climate and terrain we all know and love so well. This "difficult physical environment," Elazar writes, "led to the establishment of marginal civilization, one which was prone to seek more radical solutions to its recurrent problems." Its politics, he continues, were "dominated by issues, mostly highly moral in character." This moralism was "reinforced by a majority of Minnesota's first settlers, who stemmed from a moralistic political culture," and who, "unlike the Yankee settlers of Illinois, were virtually the first to occupy" Minnesota, and therefore "did not have to compromise their communitarian notions with any 'rugged' individualistic elements already entrenched in power."

The second wave of immigrants, huger and ultimately dominant, came directly from Scandinavia, Germany, and Ireland "to Minnesota, where they settled on virgin land. Thus, unlike their compatriots who settled in cities or rural areas already occupied by others and who had to adjust their ways to established patterns, they could retain many of the basic attitudes . . . they had brought with them from the Old World. . . . They created replicas of Old World farm villages, each with its own distinctive culture." I thought of a fifty-mile radius of Minneota: the Tyler Danes, the St. Leo Germans, the Wilno Poles, the Milan Norwegians, the Ghent Belgians, the Edgerton Dutch, the Clarkfield Swedes, the Clontarf Irish, the Minneota Icelanders. "They brought with them a kind of proletarian radicalism to add to an already radical (by American standards) tradition of politics in Minnesota." Think of the Farmer Labor Party, the Non-Partisan League, the McCarthy campaign of '68, the high taxes and good social services, the disquieting un-Americanism of voting in the last twenty-five years of presidential elections. Minnesotans tackle political problems "in a spirit of communalism and political responsibility akin to that found among their fathers." Finally, "unlike . . . Illinois, politics in Minnesota consistently has been an activity open to and dominated by amateurs. This may be due to the persistence of issues as a central element in determining alignments."

Well, of course, we say with some pride. "What *other* than issues? Who *else* than amateurs?" Elazar's book doesn't throw much of a monkey wrench into Minnesota smugness.

An old friend once had pencils printed to give away as Christmas presents. They said, "Hooray for Minnesota! We never voted for Reagan or Bush or anyone like them!" True enough. We lived up to our reputation for cranky isolation from the political fashions of the eighties, until the map of non-Reagan America showed *only* Minnesota and Washington, D.C.

I remember as a boy in the fifties having a high regard for almost all the politicians in Minnesota, even those I disagreed with, and (probably under heavy influence of listening to my father curse them for crookedness, ignorance, and venality) disliking every national figure—with special contempt for Nixon and Ezra Taft Benson. But men like Humphrey, McCarthy, Stassen, Floyd Olson, Elmer Benson, Elmer Andersen, and even Walter Judd—the fierce anticommunist China-lobby man—could be trusted to speak fine direct English in complete sentences (with clauses!), to have their hands in no one's pockets, to keep their discourse to ideas and policies and away from cheap innuendo. They seemed honest, decent men of high intelligence, *public servants* in the old sense of both those words. Whether this was true or not made no difference, so long as an entire community *perceived* it to be true. It was the cement inside people's sense of themselves as citizens. "We" were not like "them," represented by fools and crooks.

In the election of 1954, the Republicans ran Valdimar Bjornson, the state treasurer and a Minneota Icelander of immense local fame and repute, against Hubert Humphrey, in those days so impregnable that if Christ himself had returned in glory to run for the Senate, the old farmers might have said, "Well, Jesus is a wonderful fellow, but I believe Hubert would still be the better senator." Although I was ten years away from voting, it created a great conflict for me. I had met Hubert at a Farmer's Union meeting at the Swede Prairie Township Hall, had shaken his hand, and gotten his autograph in my little red book (I still have it!), and had seen him moving—smiling, affable, and confident—through the crowd of farmers, remembering every name, climaxing the night with a fine tub-thumping speech ending with a unison chorus of "Parity, parity, parity!" At eleven, I thought him a great man.

But I thought Valdimar Bjornson a great man, too, having heard my parents praise him as a model of eloquence and intelligence, a world-class orator who had corralled at least two languages, Icelandic and English, and made them do his bidding at will. And he was an Icelander to boot, sure proof of his greatness! I had even been photographed by the *Minneapolis Star* getting his autograph, a fat pink bespectacled boy standing rapt in the presence of greatness signing its name.

How lucky to be a Minnesotan, I remember thinking, and to have no choice but to be represented in the Senate by such human beings. It was an election that couldn't be lost by any citizen. I have often thought of that election since with considerable nostalgia.

This flowering of political decency did indeed arise from some peculiarities of Minnesota as a place—heterogeneous, not long out of the Old Country, and mistrustful of professional politicians. Hubert was raised in a Huron drugstore, Valdimar in the back room of the Minneota newspaper, and if they lost an election, or wearied of public life, they could return happily and ably to filling prescriptions, teaching school, or writing for a newspaper. Their life was not their office, or so we thought, and so we trusted them. No one, on the other hand, could imagine Nixon or Lyndon Johnson with a real job. They were political fish who would dry up out of the water of public life. Jefferson, had he lived long enough to know about Minnesota (the place he bought), would have liked it—yeoman citizens doing their public duty with disinterested intelligence, then returning to plain life without aristocratic pretense or private stashes of public money.

Only now in this last quarter of the century have the fires under the melting pot started to homogenize (or Americanize, if you like) the majority of the Minnesota population. When I was a boy in Minneota, the kindling barely warmed the edges.

I went to a country school eight miles north of Minneota. The teacher, Cora Monseth, was a first-generation Norwegian, and spoke only Norwegian to her aged parents. Of the children, the Orsens, Myhres, Thostensons, and Kompeliens heard Norwegian, the Andersons and the Lindstroms heard Swedish, the Sturms heard German, the Van Moorlehems and Van Hyftes heard Flemish, and I heard Icelandic. Not a single child in that school had a grandfather who spoke English either well or without a heavy brogue, and every parent learned English as a second language. In the fifties, we were the first generation to have *only* English. I was twenty before I met anyone whose grandparents had been in America during the Civil War. For the citizens of Swede Prairie, the Thirty Years War between the Protestants and the Catholics had more historic relevance than the War between the States. None of our grandparents had even *seen* a Negro slave, much less owned or liberated one.

Immigration was neither so easily accomplished nor so easily finished a psychological process as we like to imagine in our more sentimental moments: on Svenskarnas Dag, Syttende Mai, Christmas Eve. We leave out the grief, the phantom pain from an amputated culture and language, the economic catastrophe, the fear and dread of poverty, the truncated souls who went under. Ole Rölvaag, in his little novel in the form of American letters, *The Third Life of Per Smevik*, has the narrator describe, not instant Americanization, but a sequence where the first generation gives up its soul, becomes neither American nor Norwegian, but endures a kind of psychic limbo between two worlds. The children make their way only halfway into the new culture, and the third generation finally sloughs off the old like a snakeskin, losing its power along with its misery and becoming, in return, something their own grandfathers wouldn't recognize.

I think Rölvaag is mostly right, but coming a generation or two after him, I've observed the process differently than he could have imagined. The Minnesota immigrant culture became a thing in itself, neither Europe nor America, though with a few toes in both, and a few surprises that neither Europe nor America would have predicted. This third culture had its own beginning, middle, and end, and its own Götterdämmerung built into its origins and structure, probably within a single century. I call it the "pickled-in-amber" culture, and my generation is the last gasp of the first wave of it in Minnesota. After me, the deluge—the real America.

Minneota, like hundreds of other towns in Minnesota, celebrated its centennial in 1981. I'll use it as an example here, not because it's exceptional in any way, but because it's typical, a regular sort of place in Minnesota terms. It was settled first by a few stray postwar Yankees, some post–potato famine Irish, and Norwegians. The Icelanders arrived soon after, and finally the Flemish-speaking Belgians, and Dutch. At the end of *one* generation, by the turn of the century, the immigration was an accomplished fact. Only stringers and strays arrived later. Starting as a chunk of empty treeless prairie at the end of the Civil War, Minneota arrived at around the current population (1,400) within about twenty years, lightning speed in human history. It boasted a two-story dry goods store, the Dayton's of the prairies and the largest west of Mankato, a brick Gothic revival school, three or four handsome churches (Lutheran and Catholic, of course), a handful of grand mansions for the newly moneyed, including a Summit Avenue–style beauty crowned with an octagonal tower room, and reputedly designed by Cass Gilbert, architect of the Capitol in St. Paul. It had banks, livery stables, hotels, a drugstore, two doctors, and a fine newspaper, the *Minneota Mascot*, that was already on its way to being one of the most influential and highly regarded small-town papers in the Midwest. The town merchants spoke English well (in addition to whatever else), and first-generation immigrant children had already graduated from Minneota High School and gone off to colleges like Gustavus Adolphus and the University of Minnesota, to begin careers as journalists, lawyers, teachers, doctors.

A Minneotan born in Iceland, B. B. Gislason, had gone off to defend America in the Spanish-American War, risking his young Icelandic hide to help acquire Cuba and the Philippines. The town survived a grasshopper plague, a drought, killer blizzards, a bank panic (1893), and a major recession. To all outward appearances, it looked a thoroughly American place, an immigrant success story, a model demonstration of tamed wilderness, quick prosperity, domestic respectability—a triumph for civilization, a proud realization of the promise of America, already beginning to melt its happy well-fixed immigrants down into the democratic soup. And yet . . . and yet . . .

In the 1990s, over a century after settlement, Minneota remains at its

turn-of-the-century size, and in this shows amazing luck for a small Minnesota immigrant town. Most have collapsed, lost population, business and
reason for existence, and are on the fast downslide to ghost-town status.
Minneota will get there, too, but it will take longer. A handful of old
people still speak Scandinavian languages badly, and a handful of middle-
aged Belgians keep up Flemish. Business life is mostly out of town. Young
people watch a lot of television and can't pronounce their ancestors'
names—if they remember them. The Big Store is a furniture storeroom,
and the Cass Gilbert house now a duplex, minus its grand curving staircase.
The boulevard elms, planted shortly after the turn of the century, arched
eighty feet high like a green cathedral over the town until a few short years
ago, when they succumbed to the Dutch Elm Beetle, leaving the town naked on its sun-baked prairie for the second time this century.

Yet the "pickled-in-amber" culture in Minneota, and in every one of
the country towns like it, had an amazing half-life of economic and intellectual energy as it peaked fast and then declined. Take the Icelanders as an
example. They arrived around 1880, the poorest and more isolated of Eu-
ropeans, their physical and mental lives still medieval. Within twenty years
they had learned English without losing Icelandic, sent children, even from
the poorest families, to college to become lawyers, journalists, and teachers,
and had begun a publishing house and a newspaper. They took citizenship,
inventing, for the first time in their history, legal family names, but raised
bilingual children who, when asked, called themselves not Americans but
Vestur Islendingur—"Western Icelanders." Few immigrants (Icelanders included) wrote many letters home; the long sea voyage was a razor cut between two worlds. Relatives left behind were as good as dead. There was
no direct dialing to the old life, no fax number, no E-mail.

Yet for the great issues and events of American history, they were a little
out of sync. The Civil War meant nothing, the Depression arrived ten years
early with the collapse of land prices, World War II meant high farm prices,
civil rights meant going to your children's weddings even if they married
Catholics or Lutherans, the communist menace had about as much reality
as it really had. Decades arrived five years late; the soporific fifties ended in

about 1965, and the counterculture lasted until five years after California freaks had shaved and joined brokerage firms.

Was Minneota really America, and were the backcountry Icelanders, Norwegians, and Belgians really American yet? Of course. They were out of social sync, geographically peripheral, politically grumpy but able to ignore politics, and economically colonized—though comfortable because of the vast surplus of riches of the country. America *is*, or was, a country of peripheries, not of centers. Minnesota is merely a clearer (because *more* out of sync) example of it. There was no large body of people in any small place who had any experience of *being* American, aside from having old citizenship certificates folded among the family heirlooms. The first generation thought, worshipped, and most often married in its own language, but it couldn't go back, and it couldn't run for president. The second generation grew up in a foreign language, cast it off either from distaste, disuse, or marriage outside the circle. By the thirties and forties even Catholic masses and Lutheran services collapsed into English. I am at the tail end of the third generation, born in World War II, who grew up among the ghosts of immigration, in which nationally idiomatic English was a matter of age, not education. Cedric Adams still announced the Minnesota truth on the radio to rural people with brogues and cousins up in the Twin Cities, but television and the economic and social collapse of village life were about to suck us into the orbit of the coasts, of Washington, of the plugged-in rock-and-roll culture. The amber around us had dried and crumbled, and now we could say "Have a good day!" with the best of them.

Here's an example of crumbled amber, of immigrant meltdown, and the way it worked in Minnesota. During my high-school days at the end of the fifties, the only sexual advice in most houses in Minneota would have astonished a modern teenager. In Scandinavian Lutheran houses, it went like this: "You stay away from the Belgians. Get in trouble with one of them, and they'll take you to the priest and make you turn. You'll have to sign your own children away to Rome. You marry one and I won't darken the church door." Presumably Belgian children listened to some similar version with warnings about lascivious Lutherans who believed in divorce, childless houses, bad food and watery theology. *Those* churches were not about to get darkened either. Since this advice floated around in the cultural ether, I remember asking my mother about its exact provisions. "Could I marry a Jew, or a Greek, or a black woman, or a Chinese?" If you can find one, she implied, go ahead. They practice birth control, read heterodox books, and don't make you sign children away into the Vatican sinkhole.

Minneotans solved the problem of intolerance promptly and in a very American way. They proceeded briskly to marry the other, while the ethnic church and family identity collapsed in on itself except as a means of passing time in nostalgic conversation. The town now has a good supply of Lutherans with Belgian names, and Catholic Petersons. The first step in becoming a real American is to accumulate strange cousins. The second, less happy step is to forget that you are connected or related to anybody. Minneota hasn't quite arrived there—yet.

But aside from its sexual and religious warnings, the "pickled-in-amber" culture, while it lasted, had amazing intellectual vitality too. Think of the writers who came out of it: Ole Rölvaag, Herbert Krause, Meridel Le Sueur, and Tom McGrath (compare their political energy with a "real" American like Robert Lowell); Fred Manfred, whose finest work is deeply colored with both the language and culture of Friesland; and Robert Bly, whose energy comes partly from his role as an old immigrant Norwegian literary circuit rider, filled with passionate Ibsenesque improving. The ghosts of that immigrant energy are faded but still alive in my own generation. It's not a bad record either politically or culturally for a harsh, out-of-the-way place with a small population. We have done all right by not quite homogenizing.

Sometimes, after elections or televised celebrity trials, or our periodic national eruptions of "America-firsters" immigrant hatred, I ask myself, What in me is not homogenized, not melted down, still pickled in amber? The Icelander immigrants gave me two psychic gifts that still operate, one useful to me and the other mostly disastrous—though honorable in a quirky way. The old Icelanders filed and categorized their fellow humans by language skills. An admirable human spoke admirable speech—precise, witty, without jargon or cliché, with nice distinction in diction and vocabulary. The old idea of a "word hoard" survived in them; the better stocked the hoard, the more armed the human. This led to a certain snottiness in daily life. Inarticulate mumbling or highfalutin cant opened for Icelanders the opportunity for lunges of sharp satire and withering disdain. They didn't do well with TV, advertising, or the usual language of national public discourse. That fierce love of language had something to do with my becoming a writer.

The second, less useful gift is the disdain for money—particularly any talk about it. An unrepaid loan gave birth not to arguments but to ice-cold, ax-sharp shunning. You simply didn't speak to people who were guilty of some possibly imaginary shabby behavior about money. To pay serious verbal attention to money diminished you as a human. You can't get rich in America with that kind of attitude, but most of the time, I'm half-grateful to have inherited it.

So what happens now? Has the old pickled-in-amber northern European culture Americanized at last? Minnesota (and by analogy, the United States) seems to me in no danger, as long as new immigrants come in to stir the pot, or to recharge the circuits of economic and intellectual energy. I'll give two examples.

I'm a schoolteacher who complains a lot about the lack of energetic curiosity in students. So many seem bored and listless with the prospect of their own lives, wanting material comfort and security more than high adventure and joyful risk. A few years ago, the college on the southwest prairies where I teach recruited a bunch of Hmong students mostly from the Twin Cities. I taught some of them Freshman English. Their language skills were terrible in one way—mistakes with articles, verb tenses, pronouns, word order; the spelling can only be described as remarkable. Yet their essays were lively and interesting. It was quite clear even through the fog of language mistakes that they had something to say, a story to tell or a point to make, and they wished me (or any reader) to understand it. Their papers had real interior energy despite exterior mistakes. They regarded written language as an instrument of human communication. If you think the previous sentence unnecessary, a self-evident cliché, or blathery ed-speak jargon, ask your local teacher, who reads student essays by the pound. From native speakers these days, teachers get mostly pages of words without much accurate observation, without the *world* in them. "You know . . ." has become an instrument of not-knowing, not-seeing, as if the technologized and shrunken planet had passed by a human brain without making much impression.

Not so with the Hmong students. I had essays about tigers on the path to the farm fields, ghosts of murdered Hmong haunting the Thai resettlement camps in the form of flickering red lights, complaints about arranged marriages, wonderful descriptions of snow from people who first saw it as teenagers. I corrected as much of the grammatical mess as I thought possible and returned the papers. The next day, the papers came back—corrected—with requests for further corrections. And these are students from sometimes illiterate families, learning to write a language their own parents cannot speak, after only six or seven years as immigrants in Minnesota. While those Hmong students will never be "real" Americans psychologically, they will bring that energy, ambition, and curiosity to Minnesota life for a few more generations, before their grandchildren, too, are plugged into the central circuits. In the meantime, I expect a good deal of Minnesota literature to be populated by hungry tigers for the first time in its brief history. That will perk things up for a while.

A few years ago, I got a phone call from a complete stranger who had read my essay called "The Music of Failure," where I express a kind of discomfort with American notions of success and achievement, and praise the old immigrant culture that I've praised here. The stranger was so taken with my discomfort that he drove to Minneota to meet me. He turned out to be a north Indian physicist who had lived and worked in Minnesota for a long time, was separated from his native Hindu culture by distance, education, and his habit of mind as a scientist and a rationalist. At the same time, he was bored and uneasy with typical Twin Cities talk of duck hunting, bottom-line deals, and "How about those Twins?" Minneota, as I described it, sounded more like his north Indian hometown than other American places.

We became friends, and have had long conversations over the years about what it feels like to be an immigrant, to be a Minnesotan, or to be an

American. I've learned a lot from him about what the inner lives of my own grandparents must have been like. He has mastered the language, culture, and technology of the modern West as my grandparents never did, but the mastery has not killed off the ghosts of 4,000 years of genetic and cultural history. You don't shuck off religions, languages, or cultures easily—they're part of your cellular life.

His aunt visited him recently and I went to meet her and eat some north Indian home cooking. The conversation was translated for my benefit. She upbraided her nephew humorously for not being married yet. It was time for the family to arrange a proper match. I thought of my uncle, Adalbjorn, who was the first of his family to marry a non-Icelander (he married a Norwegian), and my Grandfather Herman's angry question, "Couldn't you find an Icelander to marry?" She did a little schoolwork on the Bhagavad Gita (she is a teacher of high-school Sanskrit), and then prayed and chanted before dinner for half an hour. "Is it an old prayer?" I asked the physicist. He had never learned the prayer; it was not part of his doctoral work in physics, so he asked his aunt. "No, not old," she said, and then told the story of the origin of the song to Krishna she had just sung. Only from about A.D. 700. Not old. I thought of my delight at finding a gravestone from the 1870s in a Lincoln County graveyard.

Then we sat down to a north Indian feast—course after course of piquant spices, flat bread, interesting vegetables, sticky rice, and no meat. I loved it! Here I am, I thought, smacking my temporarily vegetarian lips, in the land of the steak house, eating delicacies prepared by a citizen of the country in which, not very long ago, it was a capital offense to kill a cow. When I asked my physicist friend what he did for teenage rebellion in a Hindu family, he said he went to the Muslim neighborhoods to eat meat, chewing cardamom seeds on the way home to hide his sins.

He has now taken up landscape painting as a relief from industrial physics and invitations to hockey games and walleye fishing. He rediscovered the treeless prairies and paints them passionately, but with the peculiar eye of someone who grew up looking at the Himalayas and terraced farms just to the north of his hometown. His prairies will look as different from mine as my grandfather's would have—with their ghost images of black volcanic crags, and a cold gray roiling sea. The prairies become a richer place by being observed by people with one eye pointed at each world. So does Minnesota. So, for that matter, does the United States, if indeed we've joined it yet. The un-American (or half-American) sensibility of that "pickled-in-amber" culture is the dynamo that powers an astonishing number of good things we've done as a country so far.

Abandoned Farmsites, Yuppies, Drug Wars, and Geese

Kent Meyers

On an evening darkening with rain clouds this past summer I took my family out to the farm in southwest Minnesota where I grew up. It was only the second time I'd been to the place since we sold it after my father died. The first time, the place was one hand and my memories another, and it was only a matter of pressing them together hard and well to see that they matched. But this time the land seemed to have melted and flowed in the sun. Of the four elms that had grown around the house, only one remained. The two maples had suffered winter scald and were cut down. All seven of the apple trees in the front orchard and all four in the back were gone. The west barn with its hay loft—where we'd worked so hard in the summers and played basketball at a rickety hoop in the winters, and from where we'd gazed through the wide door at the wide, green fields—had been knocked down, an insurance liability. The cattle-yard fences were gone, as was the windbreak my older brother had spent all of one summer building. The silo was gone, the chicken house was gone, the brooder house was gone.

But worst of all the entire grove had been bulldozed. Without the grove the place looked flayed. The house and garage and a few remaining build-

Copyright 1995 by Kent Meyers

ings stood in a huge and far-too-neat expanse of lawn. Anything that had caused confusion or disorder or the smallest danger had been torn down. I couldn't get any bearings. I had to place things one by one as I told my children what it used to be. "The cattle-yard fence used to be there," I said. "And next to it . . . but no, there was a field road first—and then the machine shed. And an old box elder tree in that corner." But the corner, or what I remembered as a corner, wasn't there.

As an adolescent I knew two abandoned farmsites, and they were vastly different from the place I stood in that day. They were full of tangled weeds underneath collapsing groves of trees, with saplings springing up in open spaces—dead trunks, broken branches, rusting machinery half-hidden in wild marijuana, faded buildings, mice and birds, raccoons, skunks, rabbits, pheasants. Among the order of the row-crop fields, where anything wild or volunteer was pulled or sprayed, abandoned farmsites went their own chaotic way. Nature had overrun these places, but it was a nature dominated by the trees that had been planted and by the opportunistic weeds, a nature different from the original long-grass prairie, a mix of the wild and domestic.

My friends and I entered these places on Sunday afternoons, reprieved for a few hours from the day-to-day toil of farm work. We hunted rabbits or pheasants, talked and joked, drank a few beers, listened to pigeons cooing in the decaying barns, and tramped through the tangled weeds. We hadn't told anyone where we were going and knew that no one would look for us here or care to look. We trespassed upon these places, but as members of our community—not legally, but not illegally either. The places begged the question of law. Trespass, quite simply, would have been forgiven us, the sons of other farmers, and somehow we knew it. We were allowed upon these places just as the weeds and the raccoons and the new young saplings growing in the middle of former roadways were allowed, our adolescent force as wild as these places, and as tangled, and as tame.

As a culture we tend to designate rather than name our land, and we imply through these designations how the land ought to be used and the types of activities that should be allowed upon it. We're not to kneel in a parking lot or pick flowers in a wilderness area or stroll across an open range. Having lost their designations, however, the human designs placed upon them, the empty farmsites of my youth collapsed the dichotomies that we impose on most places—legal or illegal, human or natural, public or private—and let my friends and me interpret them as we saw fit. Their meaning was now contained in the adjective *abandoned*, and the double meaning of that word, as both desertion and limitless freedom, was exemplified in our relationship to them.

Yet our interpretation was almost always one of care. I remember hearing a rumor once that a classmate had shot out the windows of a barn at one of these farmsites. I received this bit of news with disbelief, not because those windows served a purpose anymore, but because my friends and I knew, without speaking it, that these places were ours, but only for the moments we spent upon them, and that if we left them undisturbed they would be ours again when we returned. The legal owner wouldn't exercise the law, erect No Trespassing signs, and prowl by, checking.

Among acres of carefully tended rows of corn and soybeans, the abandoned farmsites with their wild weeds and decaying buildings let us enter the most intimate relationship with nature possible—the stewardship and care of the moment. Abandoned farmsites grown to weeds don't deny humanity as a part of nature, nor do they insist that human beings are only nature. They are so clearly formed by humanity—barns, old houses, dirty glass reflecting sun, rusting machinery: straight edges and perpendicular lines, things geometrical and fashioned. Yet all these human things are being taken back by the same forces that took the humans who fashioned them, and that will in time take back the wood and even the metal, and unmake the straight lines.

To enter these places is to admit yourself as part of the force that makes and part of the force that unmakes. You become part of the place itself and behave for the moment according to rules never imposed, but understood. The things we did as adolescents on those farmsites were ritual things in many ways, without practical purpose, done in spaces set apart, in time set apart, when Sunday afternoons stretched into a kind of timelessness, and nothing mattered about our activities but the doing of them, and through the doing of them we fell into the present and lived there, and were present in that present to each other and the earth.

Partly because of the time I spent on these places and their influences on me, I have never been quite comfortable with either "private" or "public" ownership of land, or with the debate, common among environmentalists, about whether humans are part of or separate from nature. I feel something askew in these dichotomies, something lacking, a richness not allowed. Luther Standing Bear, a Lakota Indian philosopher, wrote early in this century that "only to the white man was nature a 'wilderness' and only to him was the land 'infested' with 'wild animals' and 'savage' people. To us it was tame. Earth was bountiful and we were surrounded by the blessings of the Great Mystery."

The first inhabitants of this continent gave personal names to places. To name something is to both identify it and identify with it, allow it to "be" and yet establish a relationship to it. We name our children, and that name is always greater and more complex, allowing deeper and more varied relationships, than any future designation—carpenter, teacher, chairman, mother—that the child may be assigned.

A designation, on the other hand, always implies that some other designation might have been possible, and that in the future another might apply. If I say I am a teacher I imply that I arrived at this role through time and that with more time it might change. But to give my name is to imply something true and unchangeable about myself that a person can discover only by entering a relationship with me. A designation applied to a person without reference to a proper name strips the person of personhood, and a designation applied to land in the same way strips the place of "place-ness." A soybean field might as easily be a cornfield or a mall parking lot; a wilderness area might as easily be a timber-cutting area. It is only a matter of changing the designation, a matter of law and definition rather than custom and relationship.

As I was growing up, abandoned farms existed in custom and relationship, known by their names, and they, along with the Minnesota River valley, provided me with my first experiences with "wilderness." Using "wilderness" to describe them may seem a little odd, but this oddness only reinforces Standing Bear's point. We may now think of wilderness as peaceful and pristine rather than as savage and corrupt, as the Puritans did, but we nevertheless still see it as land set apart from human activity.

Although Standing Bear and his ancestors would not have been able to understand the idea behind a modern wilderness area, they would understand the idea of a sacred place, and certainly people seek spiritual regeneration in wilderness areas. Yet one of the most common statements I've heard concerning wilderness areas—and I've heard many, since I live near the Black Hills, where the debate over how land is to be designated and used is a never-ending one—is that they are places to which "yuppy backpackers" can go, areas set aside for the leisure of the elite rather than common areas of sacred retreat.

This suggests our inability to think of spirituality in communal rather than individual terms. Unless an individual's "re-creation" aids communal regeneration, it becomes mere leisure. Bear Butte, near Sturgis, South Dakota, is considered a sacred place by the Lakota and Cheyenne people. In the words of a Lakota spiritual leader with whom I have spoken, people are "put upon the mountain." They don't just go there. They are prepared, trained, disciplined, guided, supported by tradition and community. A sacred place has meaning within the context of a communal mythology and set of relationships, and individuals go to it to strengthen not only their own lives but the life of the community that has named the place.

I am myself a backpacker. I love the solitude of the mountains and don't want motorcycles roaring past my campsite any more than the Lakota people want military jets flying low over their sun dances, as happened in 1993 at Pine Ridge, South Dakota. Nevertheless, I recognize my experience of the mountains as an individual one. While I may, if I so choose, share what I have experienced or learned there, I am not put there by a community, nor do I necessarily seek solitude in order to reenter the community more deeply. No one waits for me, to help me interpret my experience.

Without a way to value land as part of our communities, we are unable to prevent the land from being controlled by those individuals with the most influence and money. Ted Turner, owner of the Atlanta Braves and CNN, has bought 185,000 acres of land in Montana, where he is raising bison and trying to restore the land's pristine ecology. Turner plans to keep the land available to archaeologists, biologists, and wildlife scientists as a resource to further understanding of history and nature. That seems quite admirable. Yet on an NBC television special, Jane Fonda spoke of how nice it is that she and Ted can "get away" from the tension in Atlanta. It is clear that Atlanta is where they really live and that they bought this place not to enter a community but to escape from one. People who have lived in Montana tell me that much of the state's prime "wilderness" land is being bought by people to whom money is no object and who make their wealth in other places—and who have, therefore, no need to establish a deep relationship to the land, with all the troubles and difficulties and uncertainties that implies, or to the community of people who have lived upon it.

In the Black Hills, which are considered sacred to the Lakota, the introduction of gambling to Deadwood has brought speculators and investors, most notably Kevin and Dan Costner, who are building an immense resort. As the price of land rises in response to outside money, property taxes rise with it. Families who have for a hundred years lived off the land by farming and ranching are finding that such activities no longer pay their property taxes. Some have had to subdivide their property, selling it at the new, inflated prices merely to pay taxes on what remains.

Our nation's current interest in Native American history and culture, as evidenced by such movies as *Thunderheart* and *Geronimo* and (I think, ironically) *Dances with Wolves*, surely springs from our sense that we are all, as the Native Americans did years ago, losing the land and our relationships to it. Nature has become a luxury, owned and controlled by individuals, that many people literally cannot afford.

Anyone could enter an abandoned farmsite, but knowledge of the places was contained by word of mouth and limited to members of the local community. Within the community, however, the places were absolutely egalitarian. Although not consciously sacred, they were places where our adolescent energy could be dissipated and fed back to us. Groves of trees have a long tradition of sacredness, capturing as they do the breath of the earth, and on the plains, where the wind never ceases and where a person is always visible, groves are especially potent in their mythical effects, in the ways they conceal and calm. Allowed to go to these places by the community, I am convinced we came back from them more reflective, quieter, and more able to turn our energy into the work that needed doing.

Wildlife biologists and archaeologists can enter Ted Turner's private preserve, and no doubt so can his friends in the media business, but Turner surely has no neighbors to whom he owes communal allegiance and whose rights to walk the land he would recognize simply because they, or their parents before them, had walked it. Yuppy wildlife biologists, yuppy archaeologists, yuppy owners of mega-media conglomerates, and yes, yuppy backpackers—more and more the land belongs to those made elite by wealth or education or physical health or even location.

The dichotomy between nature and humanity that Standing Bear finds paradoxical and that the abandoned farmsites of my adolescence collapsed and denied, is most fully realized in our inner cities. Given the characteristics our culture once ascribed to wilderness—chaotic, dangerous, be*wild*ering—it is fair to say that our inner cities have replaced in our national psyche the dark wilderness we saw when we settled the continent.

Lewis and Clark wrote that the Lakota "must ever remain the pirates of the Missouri, until such measures are pursued by our government, as will make them feel a dependence on its will for their supply of merchandise." We now supply our inner city wilderness with just enough technology and weaponry to allow the people living there to fight among themselves, and we have substituted a trade in drugs for a trade in alcohol. We maintain the important notion of a wilderness—of chaos and danger—in our midst, and we send in the cavalry in the form of swollen police forces, or the National Guard should the natives turn their violence outward.

Ancient cities allowed storage and distribution of resources, and distance from the vicissitudes and hardships of nature. With that margin, freedoms and choices about how to live became possible, and the people living the closest to nature were eventually regarded as bound to the land and having few choices in how they lived. In modern culture this has reversed: people living in the innermost cities have the fewest choices and resources, while those who have the greatest resources—the greatest distance between themselves and nature—have, paradoxically, the greatest opportunity to "connect with" nature—and to delude themselves that their encounters with nature are pure, a delusion made possible precisely because they do not depend on nature in any immediately discernible and visceral way.

Meanwhile, our frontier, like its corollary the wilderness, has moved into our midst. When the frontier had no room to expand outward, it instead, in a huge cultural diastole—because, like wilderness, it is an imagined and cultural rather than a physical and natural place—reversed itself and re-formed within our cities. Unable to know ourselves without our frontier, we re-created it in our midst, and just as the wilderness we saw when we touched these shores was a "savage" wilderness that could not be integrated with civilization, so the wilderness within our cities is "savage," and we don't know how to deal with it culturally.

This wilderness no longer lies before us where we can conquer and subdue it. Instead it is spreading outward from our center. We can put the blame for its violence on other forces and other beings, as we always have: savage Indians, lawless young black men, immigrants, drugs. But until we admit that we needed wilderness and savagery and so created them where they did not necessarily exist, we will be treating the symptoms of our disease and not its cause.

I walk about a half-mile to work every day, detouring slightly on my walk to take a path that runs along Spearfish Creek. One day, as I paused by the creek, a small animal descended the bank on the opposite side and disappeared into a pool. Eventually it reappeared, and I recognized it as a muskrat. For perhaps five minutes I watched it gather grass from the bank. A muskrat is a common enough animal, but my encounter with it was the best thing that happened to me that day. Any encounter with a wild animal is rare during the course of an ordinary day. But it is precisely because it is so rare that we have never found a way to live with the muskrat as part of our communities, that we have designated wilderness areas set apart from our lives, and often out of reach of those who need them most.

King Midas, receiving the golden touch, touched first the things he didn't value. Eventually, however, he touched what he loved and destroyed it. We may be learning to love and value rather than fear natural places. But we have for so long turned them into gold that we have come to fear our touch upon them. We haven't learned to live with them. Ironically, until we do, only those who have most benefited from the Midas touch of our culture will have access to those untouched places.

Outside the town where I now live is a high hill named Lookout Mountain. A tunnel built under Interstate 90 allows hikers and mountain bikers and picnickers access to the land—several hundred acres of prairie and wildflowers and pine-studded draws. It takes about an hour to climb Lookout Mountain, if you're climbing with children, and they're stopping to pick up rocks and seeds and flowers, and rose hips to make tea they won't drink.

You realize you're part of the community of Spearfish when you learn about Lookout Mountain, and climb it without fear of prosecution or fines. Tourists don't know about it. There are no marked trails or signs, and it isn't designated as a hiking or recreational area. There are no rules against picking flowers or throwing trash. Yet there is no trash on Lookout Mountain, and I've never noticed a decline in the number of wild roses from children experimenting with rose-hip tea. At least a few families I know have made an Easter-egg hunt on Lookout Mountain part of their tradition, and one of my friends took the ashes of his mother there and let the wind take them.

I hope to suggest here how much different Lookout Mountain is from anything identified with a designation—wilderness area, national park, hiking area. The people and community of Spearfish have established relationships with Lookout Mountain that are varied and interwoven, that maintain the integrity of what the place is, and that include both personal and communal stories. The name "Lookout Mountain" includes a history of the place and the community that named it. You can't know what the place means unless you're a part of the town, and tourists are kept from the mountain not by law but by ignorance of the community.

What makes all of this most unique, however, is that Lookout Mountain is owned by Homestake Mining, the largest gold-mining company in North America. Homestake owns a great deal of land in the Black Hills. I don't know why the company has held on to Lookout Mountain, but I suspect that it was a parcel of land lost in the company's vast holdings. The mountain was abandoned, lost in the books. Out of this abandonment the community of Spearfish developed its own relationship to the place. Customs formed—the mountain and town grew "accustomed to" each other, and these customs begged the questions of law and ownership, public and private, nature and humanity. The tunnel under the freeway is a tacit acknowledgment of the strength of these customs.

Recently, however, Homestake Mining, responding to hard times, began divesting itself of nonmining property and started paying attention to Lookout Mountain. Ed Raventon, a Spearfish writer and naturalist, proposed that the city of Spearfish buy Lookout Mountain to keep it from being developed. The city council took the proposal seriously, but not seriously enough to make an offer. Surveys are being done to determine what public opinion is, and whether people would support spending money to buy the land. Homestake, meanwhile, is saying that it wants a fair market price but would also like the town to have the mountain. And developers, doing what developers do, are envisioning cul-de-sacs and talking of possible entrance routes.

I think everyone in Spearfish understands, to some extent, what a disaster it would be to have Lookout Mountain designated "residential"—or to have it designated anything at all. It would cease to be Lookout Mountain, and Spearfish would in a very real sense cease to be Spearfish. It remains to be seen whether the community has the love of place that will allow it to make the economic sacrifices needed to keep the land in its old communal relationship.

I don't know whether communities can overcome the forces of individualism and the marketplace to establish communal relationships to land, but I think that the way we answer this question will determine to a large extent the health of our environment, our emotional well-being, and the quality of our communities in the future. We tend right now to treat these things separately, to put someone into therapy for psychological problems, to treat the land and air for environmental problems, to call upon social workers and law enforcement for social problems. We've forgotten how to integrate these things, forgotten that they need to be integrated, that they all influence and affect one another.

In most non-Western cultures, including those of the original inhabitants of this continent, "tradition" amounted to a study of this very integration, and the elders of the community, those who had lived long enough to absorb this incredibly complex subject, were the community's "therapists"—addressing not the individual alone, but the individual's relationships to the community, the community's to the environment, the environment's to the individual, and so on. Instead of putting this study at the pinnacle of learning and deferring to those who know something about it, we have elevated the study of narrow fields rather than the study of relationships between them, just as we have chopped land up into narrowly defined designated spaces that can be bought and sold by individuals regardless of the community's health or traditions.

Yet I think a case like Lookout Mountain shows how paramount those traditions can still be, even in this modern age. Having worked on land all of my youth, having had it shape how I thought and moved, slept and woke, and related to my family and friends, having roamed it in my free time, the only form of play I knew, having felt the intense care of private ownership but also the ease of crossing boundaries in the community where I was known—and then having had these experiences magnified by the loss of that land through the early death of my father—I have come to mistrust solutions to our various problems that don't include a consideration of land and the communities upon it. I don't believe we can be psychologically healthy and environmentally diseased, any more than I believe a "virtual" community flickering on computer screens is a real community. Where is the smell of dirt in it? Where are the children picking rose hips?

All over this country, I suspect, relationships between communities and places exist that are similar to that between Spearfish and Lookout Mountain, though I think we often fail to recognize them. The land I grew up on in southern Minnesota used to be dotted with sloughs. Almost every farm had at least one slough, a marvelous place full of frogs and ducks, and great, calling flocks of geese in the fall. Some of the most powerful memories of my childhood are of those flocks, of trying to sneak up on them and how, when they discovered me, they rose with water in their wings, dripping and shining and crying, and making the whole land—my farm, my place—wild. Gradually, however, farmers—my father one of the first among them—began to tile their land, draining these small wetlands. The flocks diminished, and the colonies of muskrats disappeared.

From an individual perspective, of course, it makes sense to drain a wetland. In truth, you can hardly afford not to. It's that much more land, on which you're paying taxes anyway, that can be put into production. But the country of my youth has been diminished in its richness, wilderness and variety by the disappearance of these places. It is a community concern, and requires community solutions. I have to wonder why the communities didn't think to drop the property tax on sloughland once the ducks began to disappear, once they realized their children would miss out on what they'd known themselves. Why didn't someone argue for potted county roads and geese instead of smooth roads and empty skies?

We don't know how to think outside the narrowly defined relationships implied by our designations. We don't know how to think of land designated "private" as also "public" or "communal." A slough does not connote for us a relationship, does not suggest faint sound and children running from houses in both town and country to point to the sky and call to each other and their parents, and to the descending, calling geese.

Now, abandoned farmsites in the Midwest are going the way of wetlands. I knew only two abandoned farmsites when I was an adolescent, but now every square-mile section seems to contain at least one. I've driven gravel roads where the abandoned farmsites, weeds high around the houses, outnumber the lived-in ones. People are leaving the land—through choice or necessity or government policies that favor larger farms, but at the deepest level because they are individuals not tied to community and tradition, and can hence be bought out by other individuals.

But the visible abandoned farmsites, like the ones I knew, are themselves disappearing, giving way before the bulldozer. I understand the practical reasons for a farmer bulldozing an unused grove and buildings and spraying the weeds, in spite of the haven they create for wildlife. They are the same reasons he would tile and drain a slough, even though it enriches his life and those of his community, with its ducks and muskrats and red-winged black-birds and herons and egrets and frogs, and the trilling summer night noises that emanate from it, rhythmic and heartlike.

I understand, yet I believe we need to learn how to allow these small places to be, and to recognize that they are communal and even sacred places. We can legally set aside wilderness areas as public policy, and those with enough wealth can set aside their own reserves. But most people in this country need small places where human beings are allowed into and made part of the community of the natural. I'm not sure public policy can create such places, because I'm not sure they are created. Instead, they are allowed—when legal designations stop or are abandoned, and communities recognize a relationship, and choose to let that relationship develop.

My family has sold the farmsite where I grew up. I realize, without bit-terness, how transitory individual lives are. Yet if I could, I would not have the place as it now is, naked and treeless under the sky. I would prefer that it be left to decay slowly, recognizable but overgrown, changed by the wind and rain and sun. I would prefer that my spirit and breath, and that of my family, still remained caught, even in the blackest storms, in some small, still area within the old trees.

I believe there are communities across the country that, like Spearfish, are struggling with the issue of how far economic forces should be allowed to strip them of place and identity. I have hopes that these communities will recognize the primacy of custom, relationship, and name. It is too late, I know, for the place where I grew up. Before long the present owner will be unable to find renters. When that happens he will no doubt bulldoze that 130-year-old house and the few remaining buildings—and the place, as a place, will cease to exist, will become part of a field. I'd prefer—and I say it as a kind of plea and prayer for other such places where it may not be too late—that the place, with its original grove and weeds, remained, with owls nesting in the trees, hunting rabbits and mice, and fox making forays. I'd prefer to have adolescents whom I don't know but who live in the community that shaped me, joining the animals there—parking their cars where they wanted, and removing .22 rifles and 12-gauge shotguns from their trunks and, on timeless Sunday afternoons tromping around, enjoying a ritual beer or two, and then leaving the place as they found it, their activities mingling with mine, and all of them part of the nature that makes and unmakes, and the place properly named "the Old Meyers Place," and something of the story of me and my family kept in the community by that name.

Contributors

Photo by Larry Barnett

Photo by Sue Kyllönen

Martha Bergland

Carol Bly

Martha Bergland's first novel, *A Farm under a Lake*, was originally published by Graywolf Press in 1989 then reissued as a Vintage Contemporary paperback in 1990. The novel has won critical acclaim both nationally and internationally, finding appreciative audiences first in England and then in Sweden and Germany in translation. Raised and educated in the Midwest, Bergland currently teaches writing and literature at Milwaukee Area Technical College and lives in Glendale, Wisconsin, a suburb of Milwaukee. Her stories have appeared in numerous journals and magazines, and her story "An Embarrassment of Ordinary Riches" was selected for inclusion in *Pushcart Prize XII* and has been republished in Pushcart's "Best of the Last Ten Years" anthology *Love Stories for the Rest of Us*.

Carol Bly was born in Duluth, Minnesota, and currently divides her time between Sturgeon Lake, Minnesota, and St. Paul. She is the author of two collections of stories, *Backbone* and *The Tomcat's Wife and Other Stories*, winner of a Friends of American Writers Award; a collection of essays, *Letters from the Country*; and a writing text, *The Passionate, Accurate Story*. She is also editing *Changing the Bully Who Rules the World*, a forthcoming anthology of stories, poems, and essays. Three stories from *Backbone* became the script for *Rachel River*, a 1990 prize-winning film for the PBS American Playhouse series. Bly teaches creative writing in the summer Split Rock Program, in the Lifelong Learning Program of Northland College, and at the University of Minnesota.

Jack Driscoll   David Allan Evans

Jack Driscoll was born in Holyoke, Massachusets, and since 1975 has lived in and around Interlochen in Michigan's Upper Peninsula, where he is writer-in-residence at the Interlochen Center for the Arts. He is the author of four books of poems, *Language of Bone, Fishing the Backwash, Building the Cold from Memory*, and *Twin Sons of Different Mirrors*, poems in dialogue, in collaboration with William Meissner. He is also the author of a novel, *Skylight*, and a collection of short stories, *Wanting Only to be Heard*, winner of the 1991 Associated Writing Program's Short Fiction Award.

David Allan Evans is the author of three books of poems: *Train Windows, Real and False Alarms*, and *Hanging Out with the Crows*, and a collection of autobiographical essays, *Remembering the Soos*. With his wife, Jan Evans, he coauthored *Double Happiness: Two Lives in China*, about a year of teaching at

Paul Gruchow   Patricia Hampl

Nanjing University as a Fulbright Scholar in American Literature in 1992–93. He lives in Brookings, South Dakota, where he has taught English at South Dakota State University since 1968.

Paul Gruchow worked for many years as a journalist and editor for the Worthington, Minnesota, newspaper before turning to teaching part time at St. Olaf College, and eventually to full-time writing. His essays on the natural landscapes of the prairies and plains have appeared in numerous magazines and journals and have been collected in *Journal of a Prairie Year, Minnesota: Images of Home, The Necessity of Empty Places*, and *Travels in Canoe Country*. A new collection of essays is forthcoming. He lives with his family in Northfield, Minnesota.

Patricia Hampl first won acclaim for *A Romantic Education*, her memoir about her Czech heritage, for which she was awarded a Houghton-Mifflin Literary Fellowship in 1981. A new edition, with a postrevolution afterword, appeared in 1992. Hampl's poetry has been collected in *Woman before an Aquarium* and *Resort and Other Poems*. In 1987 she published *Spillville*, a meditation on Antonin Dvořák's summer in Iowa, with engravings by Steven Sorman. *Virgin Time* is her memoir of growing up Catholic and an inquiry into contemplative life. In 1990 Hampl was awarded a MacArthur Fellowship, and in 1995 was a Fulbright Fellow in Prague, Czech Republic. She currently lives in St. Paul and teaches in the writing program at the University of Minnesota in Minneapolis.

Linda Hasselstrom has been a resident of western South Dakota most of her life. Her collections of journals and essays include *Windbreak: A Woman Rancher on the Northern Plains, Going Over East: Reflections of a Woman Rancher,* and *Land Circle: Writings Collected from the Land.* She is also the author of three collections of poems, *Roadkill, Caught by One Wing,* and *Dakota Bones: The Collected Poems of Linda Hasselstrom,* and the author of *A Roadside History of South Dakota.* She currently divides her time between Cheyenne, Wyoming, and the family ranch near Hermosa, South Dakota.

Photo by Ken Norgard

Photo by Pete Crouser

Linda Hasselstrom   *Jon Hassler*

Jon Hassler is the author of ten novels, among them, *Staggerford,* chosen Novel of the Year in 1978 by the Friends of American Writers; *Simon's Night; The Love Hunter; Grand Opening,* chosen as Best Fiction of 1987 by the Society of Midlands Authors; *North of Hope; Dear James*; and *Rookery Blues*; as well as two books for young adults, *Four Miles to Pinecone* and *Jemmy.* A screen version of *A Green Journey* was produced in 1988 and shown on NBC, starring Angela Lansbury as the indomitable Agatha Mc-Gee. Hassler was born in Minneapolis and is a lifelong resident of Minnesota. Currently, he divides his time between Minneapolis and St. John's University in Collegeville, Minnesota, where he has been writer-in-residence since 1980.

David Haynes   *Bill Holm*

David Haynes was born in Breckenridge Hills, Missouri, and currently resides in St. Paul, Minnesota. He most recently served as teacher-in-residence at the National Board of Professional Teaching Standards and has taught fifth and sixth grades for fifteen years. Haynes is the author of *Right by My Side*, which was selected by the American Library Association as a 1994 Best Book for young adults. His second novel, *Somebody Else's Mama*, was published in April 1995, and he has forthcoming a collection of stories, *Heathers: A Saint Paul Story Cycle*, and *Live at Five*, a novel.

Bill Holm, the grandson of Icelandic emigrant farmers, was born in Minneota, Minnesota. He is the author of three collections of essays: *Coming Home Crazy: An Alphabet of China Essays*, about his teaching and travels in China; *The Music of Failure*; and *Landscape of Ghosts*, essays on American history with photographs of rural ruins by Bob Firth. He is also the author of two collections of poems, *Box Elder Bug Variations* and *The Dead Get By with Everything*. An abbreviated version of "Is Minnesota in America Yet?" appeared in *Minnesota Monthly*. When he is not traveling, Holm lives in Minneota and teaches at Southwest State University in nearby Marshall, Minnesota.

Michael Martone   *Kent Meyers*

Michael Martone was born and raised in Fort Wayne, Indiana, and currently lives in Syracuse, New York, where he teaches at Syracuse University. He is the author of five collections of short fiction: *Alive and Dead in Indiana, Safety Patrol, Fort Wayne Is Seventh on Hitler's List, Pensées: The Thoughts of Dan Quayle*, and *Seeing Eye*. He has also edited *A Place of Sense: Essays in Search of the Midwest* and *Townships: Pieces of the Midwest*. Prior to teaching at Syracuse University, Martone taught at Iowa State University for seven years and was Briggs-Copeland lecturer and assistant professor at Harvard University from 1987 to 1991. He also teaches in the MFA Program for writers at Warren Wilson College.

Kent Meyers was born in Redwood Falls, Minnesota, and raised on a farm near Morgan, Minnesota. He has published fiction and nonfiction in many literary journals and anthologies, including *The Best of the West, 4*, the *Georgia Review, Minnesota Monthly*, the *New England Review*, and the *Southern*

Review. His work has been twice listed as "Distinguished Stories" in the annual *Best American Short Stories.* He lives in Spearfish, South Dakota, where he lives with his wife and three children, and teaches at Black Hills State University.

Kathleen Norris is the author of *Dakota: A Spiritual Geography.* Her essays have appeared in the Graywolf Annual Series, the *Christian Century, Gettysburg Review,* the *New York Times Book Review,* the *New York Times Magazine,* and *North Dakota Quarterly.* Her collections of poems include *The Middle of the World* and *Little Girls in Church.* Since 1974, she has lived in South Dakota with her husband, the poet David Dwyer.

Kathleen Norris   Robert Schuler

Robert Schuler's poems and essays have appeared in many literary magazines and journals. He was editor and publisher of Uzzano Press and *Uzzano,* an important little magazine. Among his published collections of poems are *The Red Cedar Scroll, Axle of the Oak, Morning Raga, Floating out of Stone, Music for Monet,* and *Grace: A Book of Days.* He is also the author of a critical study, *Journeys toward the Original Mind: The Long Poems of Gary Snyder.* Schuler is currently professor of English at the University of Wisconsin-Stout in Menomonie, where he lives with his family.

Photo by Jon Van Allen

Photo by Susan Watson

Mary Swander   *Larry Watson*

Mary Swander is the author of three books of poetry, *Heaven and Earth, Driving the Body Back*, and *Succession*, as well as two books of nonfiction: *Out of This World*, a collection of essays, and *Parsnips in the Snow: Interviews with Midwestern Gardeners* (with Jane Staw). She divides her time between Ames, Iowa, where she teaches at Iowa State University, and Kalona, Iowa, where she raises sheep and goats, tends a large organic vegetable garden, and lives in the Fairview School, a former one-room Amish schoolhouse.

Larry Watson was born in Rugby, North Dakota, and grew up in Bismarck. He is the author of three novels, *In a Dark Time, Montana 1948*, and *Justice*. In addition to winning the Milkweed Fiction Prize in 1993, *Montana 1948* was named to the list of the year's best novels by the American Library Association, New York Public Library, and *Booklist*. It also received the Friends of American Writers Award for the best book of 1993 published by a midwestern writer, the Mountains and Plains States Booksellers Award for one of the year's best novels, and the Wisconsin Library Association's Banta Award for best book of the year by a Wisconsin writer. Watson lives with his family in Stevens Point, Wisconsin, where he teaches writing and literature at the University of Wisconsin-Stevens Point.